A Leader's Guide to Designing High Performing Quality Management Systems

The purpose of this book is to provide a simple leadership quick guide for designing high-performing Quality Management System (QMS) models. It focuses on QMS assessment, structure, process, and achieving outcomes through practical real-world tools, templates, and models. The test of any model is its outcomes. This book provides decades of insight – it ensures leaders that their QMS model *solves problems, achieves outcomes, sustains wins, and transforms organizational outcomes in high-risk environments.*

So, why is this topic important? In today's world, change is the new normal and only constant. In many industries, such as healthcare for example, the foundations of the industries themselves are shaking greater than at any other time in history. As change grows, so does the associated risk and disruption. How will leaders and their organizations succeed in high-risk environments without a good foundation? The short answer is they won't. The starting point for success is the QMS.

By reading this book, readers will learn:

- How to construct a well-defined QMS
- How to identify and counter common misperceptions of QMS
- Techniques to engage other leaders in crucial conversations related to QMS gaps, illusions of success, perceived and real shortcomings, and measures of success
- How to conduct a basic and advanced assessment of QMS models to determine what is working, what is not working, and high-risk areas to improve
- The required structural elements of high-performing QMS models
- A wholistic approach to the QMS process
- What measures constitute QMS success

A Leader's Guide to Designing High Performing Quality Management Systems

The 7 Keys that Solve, Achieve, Sustain, and Transform Organizational Outcomes in High-Risk Environments

Casey J. Bedgood

Routledge
Taylor & Francis Group

A PRODUCTIVITY PRESS BOOK

First published 2024
by Routledge
605 Third Avenue, New York, NY 10158

and by Routledge
4 Park Square, Milton Park, Abingdon, Oxon, OX14 4RN

Routledge is an imprint of the Taylor & Francis Group, an informa business

ISBN: 978-1-032-77867-9 (hbk)
ISBN: 978-1-032-77865-5 (pbk)
ISBN: 978-1-003-48513-1 (ebk)

DOI: 10.4324/9781003485131

Typeset in Minion
by KnowledgeWorks Global Ltd.

Contents

About the Author

 **Casey J. Bedgood** is an author, thought leader and master change agent with over 20 years of healthcare leadership experience. He is the author of *The Ride of a Lifetime, The Ideal Performance Improvement Eco System, The ABCs of Designing Performance Improvement Programs, Conquering the Giants, The Power of Organizational Knowledge, Fit for the Fight* and *The Mystery of Leadership*. He is a Six Sigma Black Belt and accomplished author. Over the years, Casey's work has been recognized, sourced and modeled by National and Global best practice organizations in the healthcare industry and beyond. He has amassed a portfolio of dozens of publications on topics such as thought leadership, knowledge transfer, performance improvement, strategic design, innovative thinking, transformation, Quality Management System (QMS) and many others. Subsequently, many large complex healthcare enterprises across the United States, Canada, United Kingdom and Singapore have sourced and sought-after Casey's thought leadership expertise.

Casey earned a BBA Magna Cum Laude from Mercer University and a Masters of Public Administration from Georgia College & State University (GCSU). He is a IISE Lean Green Belt, Six Sigma Green Belt and Six Sigma Black Belt. Also, CAP trained via GE, a member of the American College of Healthcare Executives (ACHE) and member of the Institute of Industrial and Systems Engineers (IISE).

Introduction

The genesis of this book is over two decades of experience working with leaders that struggle with the concept of QMS. Often, leaders fail to understand this concept, implement ineffective QMS models and subsequently are disrupted from their roles. More important and even more impactful are the consequences a poorly designed and executed QMS model has on organizational stakeholders including customers.

The purpose of this book is to provide a simple leadership quick guide for designing high performing QMS models. This guide will focus on QMS assessment, structure, process and achieving outcomes through practical real-world tools, templates and models. The test of any model is its outcomes. This book will provide decades of insight so leaders ensure their QMS model *Solves Problems, Achieves Outcomes, Sustains Wins and Transforms Organizational Outcomes in High-Risk Environments.*

The intended audience for this book includes, but is not limited to top executives, governance members, leaders of any rank, thought leaders, strategists, students, performance improvement leaders, changes agents, teachers and anyone interested in quality, improvement, strategy and leadership. Regardless of role, organization type or industry, quality matters and is a focal point for customers. Thus, those leading the charge for excellence in this arena must have a good structure, process and measurable outcomes sustained over time.

So, why is this topic important? In today's world, change is the new normal and only constant. In many industries, such as healthcare for example, the foundations of the industries themselves are shaking greater than any other time in history. As change grows, so does the associated risk and disruption. How will leaders and their organizations succeed in high-risk environments without a good foundation? The short answer is they won't. The starting point for success is QMS.

This book was spawned from a conversation I had with several top-quality leaders in the healthcare industry. The leaders of the organization had a very large footprint, served hundreds of thousands of customers annually and struggled with the value equation. In simplest terms, the value equation is comprised of service, cost and quality. It's important to note that there are arguably more attributes of value. But, we will start here.

During the conversation, the top leaders described a multiyear operational downturn. Their organization was restructured a few years back. Since the changes, the enterprise's value proposition and operational outcomes took a nosedive. The leaders were at an impasse and could not pinpoint the root cause of their issues.

The leaders were asked several questions during the ice breaker conversation. What does your governance model look like? The leaders were stunned by the question and began to describe the organization's governing board structure focusing mainly on the board.

The leaders were again asked what does your governance model look like? Can you produce a single slide (PowerPoint) outlining who is responsible for what, what are your accountability mechanisms across the enterprise, how communication occurs vertically and horizontally, how you improve and the like? Again, the leaders were stunned and could not produce a simple overview of these attributes.

After reviewing the organization's data correlated to value, the top leaders were asked a simple question. Your governance model and QMS are missing an improvement arm, what are your plans for PI (i.e., performance improvement)? One of the top leaders paused and said, 'I don't know what you mean. Are you referring to physician incentives?' The response was no, improvement practitioners trained in some methodology like Lean, Six Sigma or others that can help solve your quality, service and cost issues.

This simple example is one of so many conversations over the years where leaders had to learn the hard way that ignorance is never bliss. What leaders and their organizations don't know will eventually harm them, their stakeholders and customers. Unfortunately, too many leaders don't learn this important lesson until it's too late.

In **A Leader's Guide to Designing High Performing Quality Management Systems**, readers will learn the following: how to construct a well-defined QMS, how to identify and counter common misperceptions of QMS, techniques to engage other leaders in crucial conversations related to QMS gaps, illusions of success, perceived and real shortcomings and measures of success, how to conduct a basic and advance assessment of QMS models to determine what is working, what is not working and high-risk areas to improve, the required structural elements of high-performing QMS models, a wholistic approach to the QMS process and what measures constitute QMS success.

At the end of the day, leaders and their organizations succeed or fail based on the outcomes that are achieved. Effective leaders are those who understand their risk, plan ahead, solve problems, mitigate risks, sustain wins and transform organizational outcomes in high-risk environments via a well-defined and functional QMS model. Their counterparts quickly become the center of focus for the next case study or book.

1

Common Misperceptions of Quality Management System (QMS)

DEFINITION OF QUALITY MANAGEMENT SYSTEM

The million-dollar question to be answered is, 'What is a Quality Management System or QMS model?' In layman's terms, a QMS is a system comprised of people, structure and process aimed at meeting and exceeding customer requirements. Per the American Society for Quality (ASQ), a QMS is 'a formalized system that documents processes, procedures, and responsibilities for achieving quality policies and objectives.'

Some may be familiar with the ISO 9001:2015 methodology. By definition, ISO 9001:2015 is essentially a QMS and outlines conditions for the concept. There are several operating foci for a QMS per ISO 9001:2015. These ideals can be viewed in Figure 1.1. Some often refer to these ideals as core elements as noted in the figure. [1]

First, a QMS requires a customer focus. Ideally, the customer is the main focal point of all QMS activities. It's important for leaders to identify the term customer. Do you know who your customers are? Do you know what they desire? Do you know what value means to your customers?

A customer can be defined formally as, 'one that purchases a commodity or service.' [2] In layman's terms, a customer is essentially anyone that touches the organization. In healthcare, for example, the term customer is a complex consideration. The direct customer is obviously the patient.

However, there are other customers or stakeholders worth noting. Leaders, staff and physicians are customers here. Also, communities,

DOI: 10.4324/9781003485131-1

Customer Focus	• Primary focus is to meet and exceed customer requirements
Leadership	• Top-down leadership involvement, engagement and ownership in all ISO 9001 activities
Engage People	• Engage people at all levels of the organization to create and deliver value
Process Approach	• Use a process approach to ensure consistent and predictable results as a system
Continuous Improvement	• Create, foster and grow a culture of daily continuous improvement
Evidence Based Decision Making	• Base decisions on fact and data analysis for desired results
Relationship Management	• Manage internal and external relationships for sustained success

FIGURE 1.1
Seven core elements of ISO 9001:2015.

partners and even competitors may be considered customers in some instances. Are family members of the patient a customer? Absolutely, yes.

What about supply chain vendors, regulatory agencies and government entities? This too is a simple yes. The point is leaders should create an exhaustive list of anyone or any entity that touches their organization. Then, understand what each customer wants, what their perspective of value is and what is needed to meet and exceed their expectations.

The second core element of QMS as noted in Figure 1.1 is leadership. In order for a QMS to work properly, top leadership must be involved, engaged, present and champion the model. Leaders must also own outcomes, deliverables and be accountable to self. Another success factor is if leaders understand the QMS concept, can speak about its main functions and present their specific QMS model at a moment's notice to others if asked. If not, the QMS is likely to not succeed long-term.

The third core element of a QMS or ISO 9001:2015 relates to people. Here, leaders engage people at all levels of the organization. The activities may include foci on risks, outcomes, improvements or anything that will create and deliver value for stakeholders. The key is that QMS will not be effective without people.

The fourth core element of QMS is process. A process is 'a series of actions, motions or operations leading to some result.' [2] In simplest of terms, a process is a step-wise structure to get from one point to another. The key here is that a QMS utilizes a process approach for success. The process will ensure outcomes are consistent and predictable.

Next, a viable QMS model focuses heavily on improvement. There are several types of improvement worth noting. The first is 'old school' continuous improvement where waste tends to be the focus of choice. Waste is essentially anything a customer is not willing to pay for. [3] Common examples may include errors, defects, reworks, non-utilized talent and the like. [3] The key is that waste is bad and must be eliminated at every turn. Here, leaders and improvement practitioners focus on incremental change. Methodologies such as Lean, Six Sigma and others are leveraged to identify issues or waste and resolve them.

Improvement may also include performance improvement. This concept is more of a system view of improvement. Here, leaders focus on people, structure and process. People are important to all facets of an organization's operating canvas. Leaders in the improvement process assess people for engagement, alignment to the organization's culture, turnover, vacancy rates and many other attributes too numerous to address here. The takeaway is that improvement is next to impossible without people that are present, engaged and committed to improving the current state.

Performance improvement also encompasses structure. This depends on the size, scope and complexity of the organization or issue at hand. Common aspects of structure may include technology, the organizational chart, the functional chart, communication channels and the like. Without the proper structure, improvement will be very difficult here as well.

The third leg of performance improvement is process. As previously noted, this correlates to continuous improvement and the focus on process-related waste. It tends to be a step-wise or incremental process that is often slow to realize change or improvement. A good process or lack thereof will also determine the degree of improvement that is achieved.

The final aspect of improvement is often referred to as transformation. Here, leaders quickly make the future state very different from the current state. Common descriptors of transformational improvements relate to speed to execution, radically different, explosive or lightning speed. The key here is to move quickly, realize sustainable outcomes and make the future very different from today.

The next aspect of QMS is decision-making. ISO 9001:2015 requires leaders to make evidence or data-driven decisions. In a viable QMS model, thought, feeling or emotion are null and void. Leaders must master data to understand the process as to what is working and what is not. This level of decision-making will prevent knee-jerk reactions if not warranted and allow leaders to know when it's appropriate to act.

The last core element of a QMS is relationship management. Managing relationships is different from playing politics. Often leaders miss the mark as they fail to properly understand this aspect of QMS. Leaders must master the art of managing both internal and external relationships to ensure success will be achieved, sustained and replicated in other areas.

Let's take a more granular look at QMS defined. See Figure 1.2 for details.

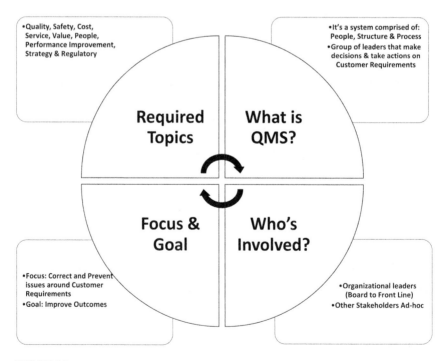

FIGURE 1.2
QMS defined.

Here, there are four aspects to define QMS in further detail. We have already lightly touched on the first quadrant. What is QMS? As noted QMS is a system of people, structure and process focused on meeting and exceeding customer requirements. In the QMS process, leaders use evidence to make decisions and take actions on any items that would detract value from the customer experience. The key is that QMS should be active, focused and not a passive report out session.

Second, let's answer who is involved. So, leaders often ask, who should be involved in the organization's QMS? The simplest answer is anyone responsible for areas that impact the customer directly or indirectly. This can range from front-line leaders or stakeholders to the governing body members. Again, organization scope, complexity and footprint will play a major role in minutely defining the QMS structure.

Third, what's the ideal focus or goal of a QMS? The ultimate goal is to improve outcomes that impact the customer. Again, the customer may include many stakeholders both inside and outside the enterprise. Thus, leaders must artfully and carefully define their customer base.

In tandem to the goal, the focus of a QMS is to correct and prevent issues that impact customers. The main focal point here is to prevent. Once issues occur, the QMS leverages evidence, process and relationships to solve the problems quickly. But, a proactive QMS is much better than a reactive one.

Finally, leaders often ask what topics are required for consideration in the QMS? The short answer is it depends on industry as well as the size, scope and complexity of the organization. But, there are some common denominators that all organizations should focus on. These may include, but not be limited to quality outcomes, safety issues, costs, customer satisfaction, people as it relates to the organization's talent, value, improvement, strategic imperatives and any regulatory items of importance. For QMS to be right focused, leaders must really know their business, their customer base and identify focus areas that impact them all.

Figure 1.3 provides more granular detail as to the purpose of QMS.

As noted in the diagram, a viable QMS model identifies opportunities for improvement. These opportunities may include, but not be limited to regulatory non-conformities identified by internal stakeholders or external accreditation organizations. Also, non-goal attainment, risks and other opportunities such as waste apply here.

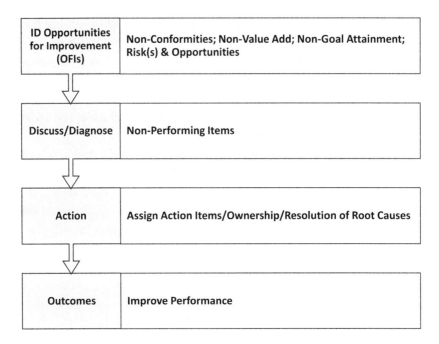

FIGURE 1.3
Purpose of QMS.

QMS leaders also spend their time, effort and focus discussing and diagnosing non-performing items. These functions elevate accountability and ensure stakeholders own, address and resolve issues. There is nothing worse for leaders than to reactively address non-value add. The key is for leaders and the QMS overall to proactively identify, address and resolve issues affecting the customer base.

Third, QMS leaders act. Again, there is nothing worse than a QMS that functions as a report out session. The adages of 'nails on a chalkboard' or 'a waste of time' apply here. Specifically, leaders spend time during QMS sessions assigning action items to stakeholders and ensure ownership. They also review outcomes during and post improvement initiatives. If outcomes are achieved, then the QMS should celebrate those wins. If outcomes are lacking, then QMS leaders should pivot and find the right solution. If not, the QMS's viability, effectiveness and credibility will be jeopardized.

The QMS process (from a high-level perspective) is also worth noting here. See Figure 1.4 for details. The process tool here is a SIPOC. [3] A SIPOC is essentially a high-level process map.

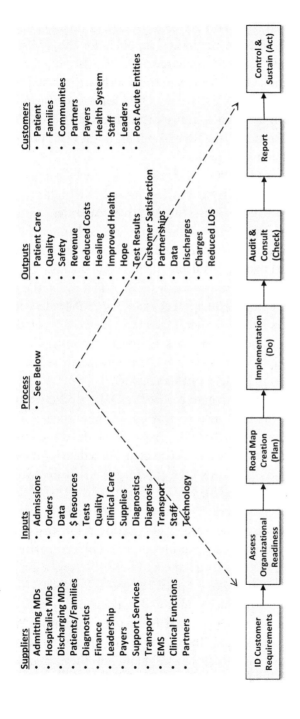

Suppliers
- Admitting MDs
- Hospitalist MDs
- Discharging MDs
- Patients/Families
- Diagnostics
- Finance
- Leadership
- Payers
- Support Services
- Transport
- EMS
- Clinical Functions
- Partners

Inputs
- Admissions
- Orders
- Data
- $ Resources
- Tests
- Quality
- Clinical Care
- Supplies
- Diagnostics
- Diagnosis
- Transport
- Staff
- Technology

Process
- See Below

Outputs
- Patient Care
- Quality
- Safety
- Revenue
- Reduced Costs
- Healing
- Improved Health
- Hope
- Test Results
- Customer Satisfaction
- Partnerships
- Data
- Discharges
- Charges
- Reduced LOS

Customers
- Patient
- Families
- Communities
- Partners
- Payers
- Health System
- Staff
- Leaders
- Post Acute Entities

ID Customer Requirements → Assess Organizational Readiness → Road Map Creation (Plan) → Implementation (Do) → Audit & Consult (Check) → Report → Control & Sustain (Act)

CTQ: Safety, Timeliness, Equity, Efficiency, Effectiveness, Patient Centered Care

FIGURE 1.4
QMS SIPOC.

Figure 1.4 outlines a healthcare example for a QMS model. The S stands for suppliers. Suppliers essentially are those that contribute to the process or supply inputs. As noted in the figure, suppliers for the QMS include physicians that admit, treat and discharge patients. Also, suppliers apply to patients and families. Often, leaders in the healthcare industry identify these suppliers as the primary customers. QMS leaders may also classify support services such as finance, transportation or other leadership as suppliers in the QMS process. The list of suppliers in the QMS process will be organization and industry specific.

The next category in the SIPOC is inputs. Inputs include any attribute that is inputted in the process to achieve the desired end. In the healthcare example, inputs may include admission, data, medical orders, tests, quality, diagnosis, staff, technology and others. The key is that healthcare is a complex arena that has many suppliers and inputs. Thus, the QMS must be an all-inclusive model that encapsulates all vital components.

The P in the SIPOC model stands for process. In Figure 1.4, the process is outlined at the bottom of the image. For example, QMS leaders begin by identifying customers and their requirements as previously noted. Next, leaders assess organizational readiness to meet and exceed customer requirements. Any gaps noted in this step are prioritized based on importance, risk and impact potential to all stakeholders.

Next, leaders create a road map to ensure the QMS is effective and efficient. Once crafted, the road map or QMS operating cadence is implemented. Post-implementation, the QMS is regularly audited and reassessed for effectiveness. Any deviations are corrected immediately. These findings should be reported up through the governance structure, while wins are sustained and improved upon.

The O in the SIPOC models represents outputs. In the healthcare example, outputs may include patient care, quality services, low costs, revenue generation, safety, healing, quality of life for stakeholders, partnerships, data and many more too numerous to entail here. The key is that inputs and process have a desired end or outputs. The goal is for leaders to ensure the outputs or outcomes produce value for all stakeholders at every turn.

The final aspect of the SIPOC process is the C or customers. We have already spent time on this topic. The reality is that an effective QMS will know who its customers are, what they want and how they perceive value. If not, the QMS will quickly fade, become ineffective and lose momentum for long-term success.

COMMON MISPERCEPTIONS OF QUALITY MANAGEMENT SYSTEM

Now that we have defined what a QMS is, let's review some of the common misperceptions of QMS. The following list is just a few of the common misperceptions leaders have posed over the years about various QMS models.

1. **Does a QMS only include quality?**
   a. The short answer is no. But, this question depends on the industry, organization and scope of business. In healthcare, for example, a QMS should focus on any activity that impacts the customer. One of the biggest pitfalls leaders succumb to in the healthcare industry is that they solely or heavily focus on the clinical side of the house. This simply means that leaders involved in the QMS model focus directly on those areas that provide direct patient care. But, what about support services such as human resources, supply chain, nutrition services and the like? Don't they directly impact the organization's ability to provide patient care? Simply put, absolutely yes. Thus, QMS leaders must include in their process any area or function that impacts the customer directly or indirectly. Otherwise, the QMS will be ineffective in meeting and exceeding customer requirements.
2. **Is a QMS a group of leaders that assembles for a good conversation?**
   a. This too is a no. As previously noted, a QMS is a system comprised of people, structure and process. One aspect of the QMS process is for people (i.e., leaders and other stakeholders) to assemble on a regular basis to identify, discuss, address and correct non-value add items. Thus, a good conversation is not a measure of success for an effective QMS as actions and outcomes take precedence.
3. **Does a QMS require improvement?**
   a. The short answer is yes. As noted in Figure 1.1, QMS or ISO 9001:2015 has seven core elements. One of which is continuous improvement. The whole philosophy of QMS is based on improving customer requirements. Thus, if improvement is missing from measurable outcomes, then leaders should reassess the QMS and make corrections.

4. **Will the QMS solve our problems with little to no effort?**
   a. Absolutely not. Leaders will reap what they put into the QMS. The QMS will only be effective if leaders lead from the front, manage relationships, leverage data for decisions, hold each other accountable and improve all the time. The key here is that each phrase is laden with action terms. Thus, leaders who lead the QMS will have to put in effort to achieve the desired outcomes. As with any improvement methodology, a QMS is only as good as what the leaders and stakeholders put into it.
5. **Is the measure of success for a QMS participants that are engaged and conduct good conversations?**
   a. Ultimately, the ideal measure of success for a QMS is meeting and exceeding customer requirements. Most leaders initially focus on value measures such as service, cost, quality and safety to start. Other measures related to efficiency and other topics tend to get added later. A part of the QMS is for people to interact. On the one hand, it's good for participants to be engaged and have good conversations. But, this is not the ultimate measure of success. If the organization is not able to meet value goals that impact the customer, then QMS conversations are non-value add or simply a waste of time.

NOTES

1. International Organization for Standardization, *Seven Quality Management Principles*. 2015
2. Merriam-Webster, 2022
3. IISE, Lean Green Belt. 2016

2

Crucial Conversation Talking Points

A crucial conversation is an interaction between at least two people. In these interactions, the topic of discussion is very important to the stakeholders. Often, the stakeholders involved may have different or competing perspectives on the topic. In short, the conversation's outcomes have the potential to impact the customer and other stakeholders greatly. Thus, leaders must approach crucial conversations objectively and wisely.

A thought leader in the service industry was invited into a conversation with another leader. The topic of conversation was the quality management system (QMS). The organization in question was a top industry performer for years. Prior to this conversation, the organization was restructured and operational outcomes tied to quality, customer service and other value metrics declined sharply for consecutive years running. The quality division was also restructured several times. The adage of 'revolving door' became the common lingo when leaders described the quality function. Leaders often left the organization from this division within a short time of their arrival.

The thought leader was engaged by the newest addition to the quality team's leadership cadre. The leader was a very competent person with reasonably high credentials. The problem was the leader had surface level knowledge at best of QMS and its attributes. When the crucial conversation began, the leaders had a light discussion on the organization's quality and customer satisfaction data over several years.

This ties back to the core elements of ISO 9001:2015 for evidence-based decisions. The data showed the organization's operational decline over the last few years was systemic. Over 80% of the KPIs (key performance indicators) were out of control. Less than 30% of the KPIs showed any signs of improvement, and goal attainment was well below 60% for all KPIs reviewed. The two leaders agreed that the organization had significant issues that were critical to all stakeholders.

The new leader started running down operational rabbit holes looking for solutions to the systemic issues. The leaders came to a disagreement on the QMS structure. The new leader felt the QMS was not the issue. The thought leader perceived the organization's issues tied directly to an ineffective QMS. As the new leader continued to focus on tactical solutions, the thought leader steered the conversation to another direction. The thought leader had enough insight to know that leaders cannot fix strategic systemic issues with a tactical focus.

During the conversation, the thought leader pulled the emergency brake by asking a series of questions. The questions focused mainly on three areas of the QMS: governance, QMS and data. Unfortunately, the new leader was not prepared for the conversation. The adage of 'a deer in the headlights' applied here.

The thought leader began by asking about the governing body. The questions following were posed to the new leader in a respectful manner.

1. Is the current structure effective? What objective evidence can you provide to support the QMS model's outputs?
   a. The thought leader was looking for improvements in KPIs tied to quality, service and other value attributes. Unfortunately, only one out of many KPIs was meeting goal and most of the others showed no sign of improvement. Also, as previously noted, most of the KPIs were out of control when the data was placed in control charts. When the leader could not provide supportive data or evidence of outputs, the thought leader progressed with question two.
2. Can leaders and stakeholders speak about the governance structure?
   a. Unfortunately, based on conversations the thought leader had with other organizational leaders' clarity on the governance structure was a major issue. Simply put, most leaders could not describe the governance model. Many leaders struggled to accurately outline who was in charge of what or how information flowed vertically and horizontally in the enterprise. The new leader was no different. They had no clarity on the governance structure that was beneficial. This led to question three.

3. Is the structure displayed in 1 slide?
   a. As expected, no one in leadership could provide a one-page schematic of the organization's governance model. Thus, it existed in theory only. This led to the next question.
4. Is the structure what is needed for today's operating reality?
   a. The debate continued between the two leaders and abruptly ended when the thought leader pivoted again. The response was significant and direct. If you can't provide a one-page summary of the governance model, if leaders struggle to describe its processes, then governance is an issue. Is short, the governance model doesn't exist in a practical format as is needed. This is one of the major contributors to the organization's current state. The conversation then shifted to another topic. The QMS model. Another list of questions was posed by the thought leader to the new quality leader.
5. The thought leader began by asking if the QMS structure was effective?
   a. Again, the thought leader was looking for data and measurable outcomes tied directly to quality scores, customer satisfaction and the like. As with the governance debate, here too the objective evidence was not present to justify the effectiveness of the QMS. This led to the next question.
6. Next, the thought leader asked if the QMS fostered or championed change? Does the QMS drive improvement or is it a report out session with minimal deliverables?
   a. The quality leader's response was quick and direct. The QMS has great discussion and some of the leaders are very engaged. But, there was no evidence of significant goal attainment, control of outcomes or improvement. Also, it was discussed that no improvement resources were directly assigned to the QMS to solve problems, orchestrate change initiatives and foster a culture of continuous improvement. This led to the next question.
7. Can leaders and stakeholders speak to the QMS process and structure?
   a. Again, the thought leader experienced firsthand that leaders across the enterprise struggled to speak to the QMS process and structure. Most leaders only viewed the QMS as applicable to the quality of services. The thought leader and quality leader agreed this was a problem and not the best focus of the QMS. The questions continued by the thought leader.

8. Is the QMS structure scalable?
   a. Simply put, can the QMS model be scaled across various business units? The current QMS model was not scalable and limited only to certain business units. Thus, areas that needed a QMS did not have access to this resource. This led to the next question.
9. Is the QMS structure displayed in 1 slide and has it been approved by the governing body?
   a. This question too received mixed results. Some larger business units had a one-pager depiction of their QMS model while others did not. Simply put, visual display of the current state was sketchy at best and not representative of the QMS structure or its processes. Stated otherwise, what was on paper did not accurately represent the current activities of the QMS. This led to the next question.
10. Is the structure what is needed for today's operating reality?
    a. The quality leader argued that the current QMS model had potential. But, the objective evidence was lacking to support this assertion. Thus, the questions continued.
11. Does the model focus on quality, operations, support services, regulatory and talent management or just mainly on quality?
    a. The answer was simple. The current QMS focused mainly on quality and neglected the other foci. The thought leader continued the inquest. This led to the next question.
12. Is QMS standardized for all business units?
    a. The thought leader was looking for agendas, meeting minutes, slides, structure, leadership representation, A3s or any other objective evidence to show the QMS was standardized across multiple business units. Unfortunately, standardization was lacking and various business units conducted their QMS differently. Thus, tremendous variation existed. The next question focused on performance improvement.
13. The thought leader asked if performance improvement resources were assigned to and available to support leaders at all business units with non-performing outcomes?
    a. The answer here was also no. Most business units had no improvement resources which were out of line with the QMS methodology and best practices.

The conversation then shifted to data and visual display. The thought leader asked the quality leader a series of questions here as well.

1. Is the right data being measured?
   a. The thought leader was looking for evidence that what was being measured was what needed to be measured. The quality leader was sure other data or metrics needed to be added to the QMS process. This led to the next question.
2. Do templates exist for displaying data so uniformity exists?
   a. In short, there was limited uniformity and templates were not adequate. Various business units had different ways of displaying their data. The questions continued.
3. Are all business units and stakeholders using run charts?
   a. A run chart is simply a line graph that displays data over time to goal. Ideally, 18 or more data points should be displayed in a run chart. The intent is to track performance to goal. For example, if the quality leader was measuring customer satisfaction monthly, then monthly data points for the outcomes would be displayed to goal on the same graph. Unfortunately, most leaders were not using run charts and did not view enough data points to provide an adequate picture of performance to goal. Thus, the questions continued.
4. Are control charts being utilized for every KPI covered by QMS?
   a. Control charts are effective in analyzing the same data in run charts for control. If the data is out of control, then special cause variation exists which means leaders should act immediately to correct the situation. Unfortunately, none of the business units were using control charts and did not know how out of control their outcomes were. Thus, an emergency was at hand but most did not perceive it due to a lack of insight. The thought leader continued the inquest.
5. Do leaders understand their data, performance and outcomes over time? Are they sharing the data with stakeholders? Is this data tied back to their individual goals? Is non-goal attainment being escalated to the appropriate senior leaders? What is the governing body doing to address non-goal attainment?
   a. The thought leader realized the answer to these questions was no as well. Data was shared in some venues, but not all. Also,

governance was not effective as many KPIs were not meeting goal or improving for a long period of time without correction. Simply put, accountability and direction were greatly missing. The questions continued.

6. What are the main focal points of displaying and analyzing the data outcomes?

   a. The thought leader was looking for three things. One, evidence, the leaders were monitoring the data to see if each KPI was meeting goal. Two, if each KPI was improving to goal. Three, if each KPI was in or out of control. This would be accomplished by utilizing a control chart. In short, the data was not being displayed nor interpreted correctly. Most leaders could not answer these questions about their QMS data.

7. Do QMS, senior leaders and governance leaders understand the data? Do they know the difference between normal variation and a crisis? What accountability mechanisms are in place or needed for non-performance? Do these leaders report their data to QMS and up?

   a. The thought leader also found issues here. Many of the top leaders and those on the governing body did not understand the data. Thus, they often engaged in knee-jerk reactions when the data was in control and failed to act when data was out of control. This led to a final question.

8. Is the data readily available to all users from front-line staff to the governing body? What common mechanisms are being utilized such as communication boards, staff meetings, performance evaluation discussions with leaders/direct reports, etc.?

   a. The thought leader learned that nearly half the organization had communication cascade issues. Thus, many front-line leaders and staff were not aware of the performance outcomes or lack thereof. So, how can leaders expect to improve if stakeholders are not aware of the issues? Simply put, they can't.

SUMMARY

So, why did we just go through this exercise? The preceding questions are a simple tool for organizations and their leaders to use as a rule of thumb when assessing the QMS. These questions represent the basic thresholds of a viable QMS model. If leaders cannot answer them correctly, then it's likely the QMS is ineffective or challenged at minimum.

In review, in order for a QMS to be effective there must be an effective governance model. The key is for leaders to prove that governance works via data. Historical trends of value metrics such as quality, customer satisfaction and the like are a good starting point. If the organization, as in the example discussed, has experienced years of declines operationally without correction, it's safe to say governance is challenged at minimum. Also, if governance is effective leaders and stakeholders should be able to explain the model and processes. It's also a good practice to visually display the governance model in one slide. If leaders cannot do any of these items, then governance is most likely in theory only and ineffective.

QMS is no different. For a QMS to be effective, leadership should be able to prove with data that outcomes tied to value have improved over time. If not, QMS and governance are challenged. Also, leaders should be able to explain and display the QMS structure in a single slide. Lack of stakeholder knowledge of the QMS is a tale tell sign that the QMS model is ineffective.

Finally, data display is a major part of an effective QMS. As noted, how will leaders know if the organization is declining or improving without good data. Simply put, they won't. Thus, data must be measured properly, displayed so all stakeholders understand it and cascaded properly. Good data and appropriate interpretation will ensure leaders know when to react and when to keep moving forward.

The key takeaway from the conversation is that it does not take a rocket scientist to determine if the QMS is working or not. Also, organizations don't always have to engage outside help when the QMS is in question. A list of simple questions and associated insight will quickly outline if the QMS is effective or not.

3

The QMS Assessment

An assessment can be defined as, 'the action or an instance of making a judgment about something.' [1] Often, leaders are asked to assess the QMS for its effectiveness, efficiency or viability. Effectiveness occurs when the QMS drives desired outcomes such as goal attainment for KPIs. Efficiency involves the use of minimal resources. Viability refers to time. Is the QMS a good or effective model now and will it be years from now? If the QMS is ineffective, inefficient or viability is in question, then leaders need to conduct an assessment.

THE BASIC QMS ASSESSMENT

The assessment can be really simple or very complex. At minimum, leaders should include the QMS's structure, process and outcomes for the assessment. The most basic assessment was discussed in Chapter 2. This is just a starting a point for leaders to consider.

Leaders can use a simple rule of thumb (i.e., a series of questions) to determine if the QMS is on track or off the rales. For review, the rule of thumb assessment focuses on three attributes: governance, QMS and data display. We won't rehash all three in detail. But, let's light review the basics.

At minimum, an effective governance model should produce desired outcomes such as goal attainment tied to the value equation. Also, these outcomes should be sustained over time with measured improvement. Leaders and other stakeholders should also be able to speak about the governance structure for the enterprise. At minimum, they should be fluent in outlining who is responsible for what, how communication flows, etc. If leaders struggle with these basics, this is a red flag that issues with governance exist.

 DOI: 10.4324/9781003485131-3

Also, as we previously discussed the QMS rule of thumb quick assessment is very similar to governance. The expectation is that the QMS model can be easily displayed in a single slide or schematic. Leaders and stakeholders should be able to connect with and describe the QMS process. Also, the QMS should produce measurable outcomes tied to the value equation and show improvements over time. If leaders struggle here, it's a good sign that the QMS needs further review.

The third leg of the QMS rule of thumb quick assessment is data display. Again, we won't cover all of Chapter 2 in detail here. But, the basics must be present to pass the exam. Here, leaders must ensure the right data is being measured, reported to leaders and visually displayed. The data should include at least 18–20 data points per KPI to paint the appropriate picture of the performance. If multiple business units exist, data should be standardized in its measurement, reporting and display. If data issues exist, it's likely the QMS needs a deeper look.

ADVANCED QMS ASSESSMENT

Strategic Planning

An advanced assessment for a QMS can and should be very detailed. First, leaders will need to assess the organization's strategic planning process. Here, the QMS leader needs a basic understanding of how the organization plans for the future. The strategic planning process should have at minimum four parts: gap analysis, planning, implementation and remeasure. Strategy leaders can assist with much of this part of the assessment. Thus, quality leaders don't have to reinvent the wheel here.

Strategic Gap Analysis

The first attribute of strategic planning is the gap analysis. At minimum annually, the enterprise should assess its internal and external operational or strategic gaps. These gaps may include a community health needs assessment in the previous healthcare example noted. This community assessment helps healthcare leaders better understand the communities they serve, who their customers are and what gaps exist in the provision of health services for their service area. Again, this part of the assessment will vary based on the industry, size, scope and complexity of the organization. But, it's a crucial element of success for leaders to know who their customers are and what they need.

Another aspect of the external gap analysis may include industry data of projections related to the book of business. In healthcare, for example, strategy firms constantly update service line data related to trends, future projections and growth or viability estimates. This data in the hands of the right organizational leader will help steer the business to the right operational portfolio. In short, part of strategic planning is to know what business to be in, what service lines to invest in and how to grow the organization. Gaps identified during this aspect of the assessment are a high priority.

Third, the QMS leader needs a good understanding of internal strategic organizational gaps. There are many attributes to consider here. But, leaders must not fall prey to the silo phenomena. This occurs when leaders only focus on the quality side of the house. To start, leaders should focus on the basics.

This internal focus related to strategy should center on outcomes and performance of value metrics. As noted value can refer to many KPIs such as quality, customer satisfaction, safety, regulatory requirements, financials and the like. Here, the QMS leader needs a simple picture of what metrics are being measured, how many of the metrics are meeting goal, how many metrics are improving and what percentage of the goals are in or out of control. This quick assessment of the top ten or so organizational metrics will provide great insight into the organizational culture and ability to succeed with QMS. The more the goal attainment and control of outcome the better. The less goal attainment indicates a higher risk of QMS ineffectiveness or failure.

Strategic Planning Process

The QMS leader then needs a basic or high-level understanding of the organization's strategy planning process. Once gaps are identified, leaders create plans or playbooks to fill the identified gaps. Here, the focal points are the goal setting process, resourcing to meet goals and desired outcomes. At minimum, the QMS leader needs to determine if the organization identifies all its gaps, sets goals to meet the gaps and budgets for resources to ensure goals are met. If the organization has perpetual roll over budgets that are not directly tied to current state gaps and goals, then caution is warranted. The greater the alignment of these attributes during planning, the lower the risk that QMS will be ineffective or fail.

Strategy Implementation

Next, the QMS leader needs a good understanding of how the organiza-tion implements its strategic plans. Are the plans immediately rolled out and implemented? Are delays in the process present? Is implementation a flawless process or are late adopters the disruptors of strategic implemen-tation. The key here is for the QMS leader to understand if the enterprise can implement change quickly and effectively. If the organization and its leaders struggle to implement strategic plans, there is a good chance it will struggle with governance and QMS as well.

Strategy Reassessment

The last part of the strategic process is reassessment. Here, leaders ide-ally reassess their strategy implementation and subsequent outcomes fre-quently. Frequency depends upon the organization, but at minimum a good rule of thumb is monthly rechecks. This ensures the plans are on track, meet the intended end and pivots occur if outcomes stray from goal.

The takeaway is that QMS is a significant part of the organization's oper-ating fabric and should influence strategy. If the organization has a well-oiled and effective strategic planning process, then there is a good chance QMS will be effective. If the organization and its leaders struggle to iden-tify gaps, link goals and plans to gaps and budget resources to meet goals, there is a good chance QMS will be dysfunctional as well. The old adage of 'leadership sets culture, culture drives quality' applies here.

ORGANIZATIONAL STRUCTURE

We will talk more about QMS structure in later chapters, but the focal point here is the organization's structure and where QMS fits in. The QMS leader should request an organizational chart of the enterprise. This is often a contentious issue as larger organizations can be very complex with complicated reporting structures. But, the QMS leader needs a clear pic-ture as to who reports to whom, where QMS fits in the reporting structure and the like. This will paint a very clear picture of accountability or lack thereof and sponsorship available to QMS leaders.

If the organizational leaders don't have a clear and well-defined organizational chart, this is a red flag. The QMS leader should expect that governance, oversight and accountability may be limited, in question or completely ineffective. This will directly impact the effectiveness of the QMS over time.

TRUE NORTH STATEMENT

A true north is essentially what the QMS should be doing versus what it is doing. This concept also applies to the organization as a whole and individual business units. For this conversation, the QMS leader needs a clear statement of the desired end. Let's use a healthcare example.

A large healthcare system has a strategic true north to be the leading teaching healthcare system for the region. In order for this to occur, the quality program (i.e., QMS) must be the national best practice site for quality and safety. Thus, the true north statement would be: 'To be the national best practice site for quality and safety.'

The key here is for the QMS leader to assess the following:

- Has a true north has been established for the QMS?
- Is the true north statement correlated directly with the organization's vision?
- Is the desired end a realistic destination or only a pipe dream?

An effective QMS will need a viable and aligned true north. If it's missing, the QMS leader has work to do.

VALUE STREAMS

A value stream is essentially 'the set of actions that take place to add value to a customer.' [2] The key here is for the QMS leader to determine if value streams have been identified, approved by the governing body (as indicated) and socialized to stakeholders. In layman's terms, QMS value streams are ways in which the QMS adds value to its stakeholders. Often, QMS models focus on values streams consisting of quality, safety, harm, regulatory compliance and the like. The key is that each value stream should be specific, measurable, goal-oriented and validated with data. If the data is not meeting goal or at minimum improving to goal, this is a red flag for QMS leaders. If value streams are missing, the QMS leader has work to do. Otherwise, the QMS will not be effective.

SWOT ANALYSIS

A SWOT is a very useful and simple tool that leaders can leverage when assessing the QMS. [3] Here, there are four parts. Let's review a few arbitrary examples. The S represents internal strengths. Strengths of the QMS may reflect readily available data, top leadership sponsorship, standardization of outcomes, good data display and the like. These are just simple examples for conversation.

The W represents internal weaknesses. A few abstract examples for the sake of conversation may be limited leadership attendance to meetings, variation in meeting agendas, variation in QMS models across several large business units, etc. The key here is for leaders to identify their internal weaknesses as it relates to the QMS. These attributes will be organizational dependent.

The O stands for external opportunities. Here, leaders may find during the assessment that QMS leaders have an opportunity for training that occurs outside the organization. There also may be regulatory requirements that need to be a part of the QMS derived from external accrediting organizations. The key here is for QMS leaders to assess what opportunities for improvement exist for the QMS outside the organization. This too will be industry and organization specific.

Finally, the T stands for external threats. When assessing the organization's QMS, leaders must consider threats to the QMS. Common considerations may include:

- Are there any competitors entering the service area that may impact the organization's ability to provide safe and effective services?
- Are there environmental factors that may impact the safety or effectiveness of services? The COVID 19 pandemic is a prime example. Here, external supply chain issues impacted healthcare organizations ability to provide services when personal protective equipment (PPE) or surgical supplies were scarce.

The takeaway is that QMS leaders need to use simple tools when conducting an advanced assessment of the QMS. A SWOT tool meets this need. Leaders must identify, understand and mitigate risks to the QMS. Some issues will be internal to the organization while others are external. During the assessment, the QMS leaders should gain understanding as to what is working and what is not. The goal is to improve what is working and fix what is not. But, how will QMS leaders improve if they lack insight on these four attributes? Simply put, they won't.

STANDARD WORK

Another assessment tool QMS leaders can leverage is consideration for standard work. In simplest of terms, leaders must consider the following:

- Does the organization have a document management program?
- Are all organizational policies, procedures or work instructions standardized in templates?
- Are all organizational documents housed in a knowledge management system?
- Are these documents readily available to end users so they know how to do work correctly and the same each time?

In order for a QMS model to work effectively, the organization needs standard work. This is accomplished by a well-organized document management program. If the QMS leader cannot see that standard work exists, there is a good chance the QMS is at high risk of failure. Thus, more work is needed to prime the environment for a successful QMS.

PERFORMANCE IMPROVEMENT

When assessing the QMS, one key aspect is for leaders to consider the performance improvement mechanism. Common considerations are as follows:

- Does an improvement mechanism exist?

- Is a common methodology used? There are many methodologies that are effective such as lean, six sigma and the like.
- Have the right stakeholders been trained on the methodology? This can range from front-line staff to governing body members organizationally dependent.
- Are trained performance improvement resources readily available to assist QMS leaders in solving problems, implementing needed changes and measuring outcomes?
- Are improvement outcomes present, readily available and significant?
- Have improvements been published and shared outside the organization?

The performance improvement structure will vary based on the organization's size, scope, complexity and value needs. A one-size-fits-all model here may not be realistic or applicable. When leaders assess the performance improvement structure, they should focus on several attributes: structure, methodology, resourcing and outcomes. The key is for the QMS leader to understand if the needed improvement arm exists or not. If not, more work is needed to develop an effective QMS. Without improvement resources, it will be near impossible for the QMS to improve customer requirements.

VOICE OF THE CUSTOMER

Part of the QMS assessment should include a voice of the customer survey. Here, QMS leaders engage stakeholders that are involved with the QMS. The goal is to gain insight as to what is working, not working and can be improved based on an outside perspective. Without insight, QMS leaders can easily become heroes in their own minds due to lack of perspective.

A simple survey can be conducted for all stakeholders directly involved with or indirectly impacted by the QMS. Again, the stakeholder list will vary based on an organization scope, size and complexity. The key is to capture as much insight as possible from the stakeholders perspective. Thus, the feedback net should be as wide as possible.

Common feedback questions may include, but not be limited to:

- What's working with the current QMS?
- What is not working with QMS currently?
- Are there any immediate concerns or burning issues not being captured by the QMS?
- In your opinion, is the QMS effective?
- In your opinion, is the QMS efficient?
- In your opinion, is the QMS viable for the long run?
- What aspects of the QMS model should be changed?
- What aspects of the QMS model need to change?
- List one thing you would change today about QMS.
- List one thing about QMS that should not be changed.

The key is for the QMS leaders to be creative and garner as much feedback as possible on the current QMS model from stakeholders. This insight should be incorporated into improvement plans to make the QMS better and more viable for the long run. The reality is simple. Often they don't know things because they don't ask. A simple voice of the customer survey is a great tool to determine the current state of QMS and what needs to be done to make it better.

SUMMARY

Overall, when leaders begin designing their QMS models an assessment should be a top priority. As with all assessments, the best starting point for gaining insight is the current state. Leaders need to know what the current structure looks like, the current process to support the structure and review outcomes to support improvements or lack thereof.

The key is for leaders to gain as much input for all stakeholders involved in the QMS process or affected by it. The more insight the better. Once the current state is defined, QMS leaders should prioritize improvement opportunities. Then, create a road map to design the ideal QMS model for their organization. Once implemented, the QMS should be measured regularly and verified with data that it's effective.

Now that a simple assessment overview is complete, let's dive into the concept of QMS structure.

NOTES

1. Merriam-Webster, 2022.
2. Wikipedia, 2022.
3. IISE, Lean Green Belt. 2016.

4

The QMS Structure

When designing high-performing quality management systems (QMS), it's imperative for leaders to ensure the right structure is in place. For this conversation, we will focus on several aspects of the QMS structure leaders should consider. The forethought is that QMS models should be tailored to the organization's needs, structure, resources and operating canvas. But, there are several common denominator QMS structural components that are cross-functional.

TRUE NORTH

As we noted briefly in chapter 3, highly effective QMS models need a vision for the path ahead. The true north is simply a statement of where the QMS needs to go from its starting point today. In short, the true north is what the QMS should be doing versus what it does today.

As noted in Figure 4.1, QMS leaders should work with stakeholders to craft a simple true north statement that resonates with all stakeholders. Think of an elevator speech. If you are standing on an elevator with a top leader who asks what QMS is, its function and desired end. What would you say? Could you craft your response in less than 60 seconds? In the figure, the QMS leader could easily convey that the desired end for QMS is to be the national best practice site for quality and safety.

The National Best Practice Site for
Quality and Safety

FIGURE 4.1
True North (Enterprise QMS).

    DOI: 10.4324/9781003485131-4

The goal is to keep it simple. Make the true north statement resonate with those that are and are not familiar with QMS.

QMS MACRO BASIC STRUCTURAL ELEMENTS

There are several basic structural elements QMS leaders must ensure are readily available. From a 30,000-foot view, leaders should be able to quickly view the structure of the QMS and governance model to ensure all required elements are there. See Figure 4.2 for details.

In Figure 4.2, the starting point at the top of the figure is strategy. Here, leaders need to ensure the organization has a strategic planning process as outlined in previous chapters. An effective strategic planning process should have four basics: gap analysis, planning, implementation and reassessment. QMS leaders must ensure the QMS model is aligned with the strategic planning process. If strategic planning is not adequate, this is a signal that QMS may have challenges. But, from a simplistic perspective the first QMS macro basic element is strategy.

The next basic element for QMS success from a 30,000-foot view is governance. This too was covered in previous chapters. But, the takeaway is

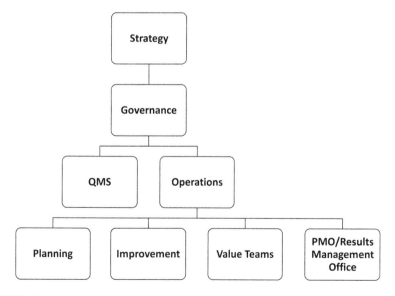

FIGURE 4.2
QMS macro basic elements.

for the leaders to understand, be able to speak about and link their business functions back to the governance model. If the governance model is present, effective and producing desired outcomes, the QMS has a greater chance of success. Without governance, QMS will struggle at best.

The next elements of focus are QMS and operations. We will discuss the QMS structure more later in this chapter. For operations, it's imperative that the organization has an operations arm that can help solve problems, reduce risk and drive outcomes. The key here is that QMS and operations must function in tandem. Thus, leadership, vision, goals and resourcing must be aligned.

Operations has many subparts. Let's lightly discuss a few of the most common operational elements. First, organizations invest structure and resources for planning. Planning can include the strategic planning process, planning for infrastructure, technology planning, capital purchases of large dollar items and many other items. The key is that the organization has leaders and resources focused on planning for the future as it relates to vision, strategy, operations and outcomes.

The second operational subpart that organizations commonly include is improvement. Here, organizations invest resources in training and deploying improvement leaders to solve issues, sustain success and implement change. The improvement model can vary based on organizational size, scope, complexity and resource availability.

The final support we will mention can take many forms. As noted in Figure 4.2, some organizations leverage a project management office (PMO). In some instances, PMOs function as scheduling, tracking and facilitation arms. Here, this function assists leaders and teams to keep track of improvement initiatives, facilitate meetings and the like. The value of a PMO to the QMS will depend upon the needs of the QMS, the skill sets in the PMO, alignment of both functions and the bandwidth of the PMO.

Organizations may also have a formal results management office. This function's scope may also vary based on organizational type, size and scope. Commonly, the results management office may be staffed with improvement practitioners, data scientists and work in tandem with communications teams. Regardless of type, the purpose is to have a bank of resources QMS leaders can pull from to identify, analyze, solve, sustain and validate outcomes. If improvement resources are missing, the QMS will stagnate and be marginal at best.

The takeaway from Figure 4.2 is that QMS leaders should ensure all the basic macro elements are present, fully functional and effective. If any of the links to this chain are missing, the QMS will be underperforming.

QMS CRITICAL FACTORS

As noted in Figure 4.3, there are several critical factors to be considered when designing high-performing QMS models. The top functions in this figure are the same as Figure 4.2. Leaders must ensure that the organization has a solid strategy process where gaps, goals, budgets and outcomes are linked or aligned. If not, the strategy process needs to be reviewed and possibly adjusted.

The second level is exactly what was described in the previous discussion. The governance model must be present, effective and relatable to all stakeholders. A simple test is if leaders can articulate the organization's governance model and display it in one slide. If not, there is a good chance governance is lacking and QMS will be negatively impacted.

The third level of critical QMS factor include QMS, improvement, targets and cultural alignment. The premise is simple. The QMS is directly involved with and must influence strategy and governance. From an

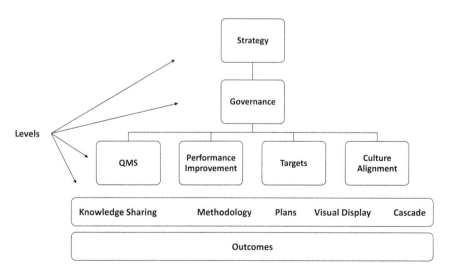

FIGURE 4.3
QMS critical factors.

intermediate level QMS also acts a filter for improvement opportunities. As issues arise and are filtered to the top by QMS leaders, performance improvement functions are leveraged to solve the issues. Also, the improvement arm helps to sustain wins and continuously improve all facets of the organization's operating canvas.

One critical factor of a successful QMS structure is targets. Simply put, what key performance indicators (KPIs) do the QMS value, target, leverage and essentially effect. Common targets may include, but not be limited to quality scores, customer satisfaction, costs, safety scores, efficiency, standardization and synergies. Here, the goal is to standardize structures and processes to achieve efficiencies. Also, working collaboratively QMS leaders must leverage the structure and process to align culture.

Culture is simply the way work gets done in an organization. People do the work so they are the bearers of organizational culture. The key is that culture is the single most important determinant if the QMS or other improvements will succeed or fail. Thus, QMS leaders must align culture to ensure the model is effective, efficient and viable long-term.

The fourth level QMS critical factors worth noting are knowledge sharing, methodology, plans, visual display and cascade. We have touched on these in previous chapters, but will lightly discuss again here. Let's start with knowledge sharing. Knowledge sharing is synonymous with knowledge transfer.

Knowledge transfer occurs when knowledge is passed from one person to another. Also, QMS leaders should consider a more global perspective. How is knowledge transferred from department to department, from division to division, across the enterprise and externally? The key is that knowledge sharing has two aspects: internal and external.

Internal knowledge sharing occurs inside the organization regardless of scope or impact. In contrast, external knowledge transfer is sharing knowledge, best practices, improvement wins or innovative ideas outside the organization. High-performing QMS models participate in all the above. In these models, leaders and their organizations may focus on several tactics such as succession planning, cross-training, coaching, mentoring, knowledge management systems and the like. High-performing QMS leaders also tend to share knowledge externally as well. Here, they may publish improvement wins in industry best practice venues, present at national conferences and the like. The key is to ensure knowledge exists, is transferred and leveraged to improve.

As previously noted, methodology is a critical factor for a high-performing QMS. The base methodology leaders can start with is ISO 9001:2015. By definition, ISO 9001:2015 is QMS. Other supporting methodologies may include Lean or Six Sigma.

Lean focuses mainly on eliminating process related waste. This concept is centered around a basic four-step process: current state, identify waste, future state, continuously improve. [1] In layman's terms, improvement practitioners leverage lean to outline the current-state operating environment, identify waste such as delays, errors, reworks and the like, create a much more efficient future state and then improve all the time.

QMS leaders may also leverage Six Sigma. This methodology focuses heavily on reducing variation. It's a data-driven perspective leveraged to increase efficiency and outcomes. Irrespective of methodology selected, QMS leaders need a base methodology to ensure the QMS is effective, efficient and viable for the long run.

Plans are also a major aspect of ensuring a viable QMS model is developed. These plans may include strategy or vision as previously discussed. Other common plans may include communication plans, change plans, improvement plans, talent plans and the like. The takeaway is that planning is a major piece of the QMS puzzle. A well-crafted planned portfolio will ensure QMS stands the test of time by delivering the desired end of meeting and exceeding customer requirements continually.

Visual display is also another QMS critical factor. Here, leaders must ensure the metrics selected are displayed so all stakeholders understand them, can access them and know when performance is improving or not. In hospitals, for example, it's common for QMS leaders to leverage communication boards in work areas for each department. A simple cork board that fits the available space is placed in common areas where staff and leaders pass by during their work routines. The premise is simple. Consider a simple hospital example. Display each major KPI such as infection rates, falls, mortality and other measures over time to goal. A simple and effective tool is a run chart or line graph. We will discuss this concept in later chapters.

When leaders view the data, there are three questions to be answered: are we meeting goal, are we improving to goal and are outcomes in or out of control. The last consideration will require a control chart and basic knowledge of statistical process control. This is where the results management office or Six Sigma black belts can benefit the QMS. Irrespective of the method used, data representing QMS should be displayed so all stakeholders can access it and understand the current state.

Communication cascade is also a critical factor of QMS success or failure. Here, leaders should craft a communication plan outlining how information will be shared to stakeholders. Again, stakeholders may include front-line staff up to the governing board in some larger organizations. In its simplest form, QMS leaders must ensure communication travels through both vertical and horizontal channels.

Vertical communication occurs when leaders share information up and down the organizational chart. In contrast, horizontal communication occurs when leaders share information across business units for example. The key is for leaders to ensure QMS information reaches desired stakeholders, resonates with their work and provides direction as to the road ahead. If the communication is inconsequential or unrelatable to recipients, the adage of 'falling on deaf ears' will apply. The takeaway is that QMS leaders must ensure a communication plan exists. If not, the QMS will be limited.

Finally, the last layer of QMS critical factors is outcomes. If I had a nickel for every time I have heard senior leaders ask when will outcomes improve, the adage of 'richer than Fort Knox' would be applicable. The reality is that outcomes are a derivative of all the other critical factors. Leaders should not expect a high-performing QMS or to solve major challenges related to value if the other components are not aligned or present.

The reason we traversed through an overview of Figure 4.3 is to provide QMS leaders a simple schematic or rule of thumb to quickly prepare the organization for success. Leaders should always start with the basics when designing QMS models. First, ensure the strategy process is present, effective, efficient by linking gaps, goals, budgets and outcomes.

Second, leaders must influence the organization's governance structure to ensure it exists. Also, all stakeholders should be able to speak on its existence, structure, process and reporting mechanisms. If leaders can't speak on the governance model, then it really doesn't exist.

Third, QMS leaders must ensure QMS, improvement, targets and culture are aligned. If any of these critical factors is missing, the QMS is likely to be ineffective.

Fourth, leaders need to share knowledge both inside the organization and externally. How would a QMS model be a best practice if it doesn't share knowledge, best practices, innovative concepts and the like? Simply put, it won't. The QMS should also be designed to encompass methodology, various plans, data display that is customer friendly and good communication practices.

At the end of the day, outcomes should be the last concern for top leaders and governing body officials. For those who understand the concept of QMS, asking about outcomes first is same as putting the cart before the horse. Simply put, outcomes will be achieved if the other critical factors are present, effective and aligned first.

QMS CHARTER

One of the most basic, but critical structural component of a high-performing QMS model is the charter. Before any work is actually done in the QMS, leaders must begin with the charter. It's important to note that charters can take on several forms. As noted in Figure 4.4, the chart begins with the true north statement at the top. As discussed, QMS leaders must define what the QMS should be doing that is different from what it is doing today.

Next, QMS leaders establish the goal statement. This statement is essentially a declaration of what the QMS leaders want to achieve via QMS.

True North Statement			
• *The National Best Practice site for Quality and Safety*			

Goal Statement	Timeline		
• Create a standard QMS model applicable for all business units	**Phase**:	**Planned Completion Date**	**Actual**
• Be a national leader in the quality and safety space	**Define**	Add info	Add info
• Standardize the QMS process and outcomes across business units	**Measure**		
	Analyze		
• Meet all QMS regulatory requirements	**Design**		
	Control		

Business Case & Benefits	Team Members		
• Improve Safety, Quality & Outcomes	**Position**	**Person**	**Title**
• Contribute to the industry body of knowledge			
• Transform the industry's accreditation persona	• Team Lead	Add info	Add info
• Realize synergies in accreditation, safety and quality	• Sponsor		
• Share knowledge nationally	• Process Owner		

Scope	
In Scope: Business Unit 1, 2 and 3	• Member
	• Member
	• Member

Out of Scope: None

FIGURE 4.4
QMS chapter sample.

The goal should be specific and realistic. In the example in Figure 4.4, there are several goals for discussion. The QMS leadership intend to create a standardized QMS model that is applicable for all business units. The QMS structure and scope will depend on the organization's size, scope, complexity and geographic footprint.

Also, the team intends for the QMS to help the organization to be a national leader in quality and safety. This will occur by standardizing the QMS structure, process and outcomes. Moreover, the QMS will be leveraged to ensure the organization is in compliance with all regulatory requirements for the industry.

Next, the leaders outline the business case and benefits. This essentially answer what will be gained by the new QMS model. In the figure, the exemplary benefits include attributes such as improving safety, quality and overall value outcomes. Also, the benefit of the QMS model will be contributing to the industry body of knowledge via sharing best practices, wins and innovative ideas. Finally, the organization will benefit by gaining synergies between accreditation, quality and safety functions.

One of the simplest and often overlooked aspect of the charter is the scope. The scope outlines the boundaries of the QMS. Will the QMS be applicable to all business units or just some? A well-defined scope will ensure the organization uses its time and resources wisely instead of trying to boil the ocean which can be overwhelming and non-productive. For the example in Figure 4.4, the scope includes business units 1, 2 and 3. Leaders will need to thoughtfully craft the scope of the QMS to ensure success becomes a reality.

The next step in design is for QMS leaders to outline the timeline and process for the QMS model implementation. Here, leaders list the major tollgates from discovery to controlling change and outcomes. We will discuss the process more in a later chapter. But, the takeaway is that QMS leaders must have a solidified process and timeline for relevant tollgates. If not, the QMS design may stagnate, lose support from stakeholders and ultimately fail.

The final aspect of the QMS charter is to determine who will be involved and what their obligations are to the QMS. Again, the size, scope and complexity of the organization will affect the QMS leadership cadre, team members and attendees. But, leaders must identify roles and share expectations so the QMS is effective.

In the end, the purpose of the charter is simple. It provides a written contract (of sorts) outlining the vision, goal, benefits, scope, process and timeline for QMS design. Moreover, the charter formally connects QMS leaders and stakeholders to tangible responsibilities. These attributes are all very important for designing and implementing an effective, efficient and viable QMS.

QUALITY MANAGEMENT SYSTEM STRUCTURE

Here is a simple disclaimer before we begin the discussion on QMS model structures. There are various models that work. The QMS leaders will have to select the QMS model that best fits their organization's needs, operating canvas and culture. But, there are several basics that all QMS models should have in common.

As noted in Figure 4.5, there are four basic attributes of a QMS structure. More discussion on this topic can be found in *The Ideal Performance*

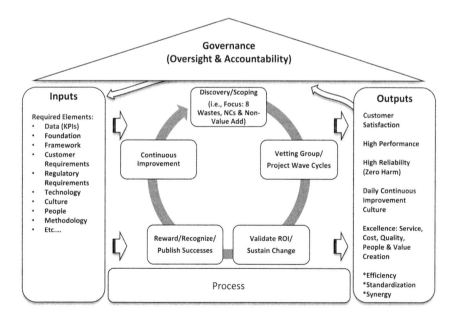

FIGURE 4.5
Basic quality management system structure.

Improvement Eco System (Bedgood, Casey 2021). To start, QMS leaders must ensure inputs are present and representative of the organization's current state. Inputs can also be referred to as required elements.

Inputs include attributes such as people, knowledge, skill, data, foundation, framework, regulatory requirements, technology, culture, methodology and others. Inputs can also include strategic imperative or guiding objectives that the governing body has established to guide the enterprise forward. Goals and objectives also apply here. Ideally, each year organizational leaders establish strategic, operational and tactical goals for the enterprise. These will play a major role in the success or failure of the QMS. Thus, inputs are a very first step in designing the QMS.

Next, a QMS has a process as noted in Figure 4.5. The process may vary from one organization to another. The figure outlines a simple continuous improvement process. The process includes a discover or scoping phase. Here, leaders look for waste such as errors, reworks and the like. They also scope out any regulatory requirement deficiencies, non-goal attainment or other value add that would prevent the organization from meeting customer requirements.

Once opportunities are identified, they are 'tossed' into the performance improvement cycle. Some may refer to this aspect of the QMS process as the wave cycle. In simplest of terms, anything not meeting goal or regulatory requirements is sent through a vetting group to validate its priority, risk and 'worthiness' of resource commitment. The vetting group is a group of highly skilled leaders that vet each improvement opportunity identified by the QMS process.

Often, vetting group membership may include a black belt, project managers and various leaders from quality, talent management, finance and customer experience to start. The vetting group makeup may change over time based on the organization's priorities or resource availability. The key here is to ensure a leader representing each aspect of the value equation is present, engaged and accountable to the QMS.

After vetting occurs, non-performing outcomes are improved and the return on the investment (ROI) is validated. Validation of ROI should occur by a leader external to the process. Typically, organizations may select the financial leader of the organization for example to give their stamp of approval on all cost savings improvements. The type of ROI may vary from improvements in harm or safety to millions of dollars in hard savings due to waste reduction. This validation arm adds another layer of credibility to outcomes.

After top leaders agree on what is improved, leaders must magnify wins and celebrate team success. Reward mechanisms may include presenting the favorable outcomes to the governing board, top leaders or even outside the enterprise in industry best practice venues. Other reward mechanism may include financial incentives, promotions, stretch assignments and others. The key is for QMS leaders to recognize and celebrate success real-time and at every turn. Don't miss an opportunity to reward effectiveness.

After the improvements are validated and rewarded, the QMS leaders must ensure a process is in place to continuously improve. One step could be to leave the focus area on the QMS agenda for a period of time in a monitoring format to ensure wins are sustained and even improved further. The last thing QMS leaders need to do is to see an initial improvement, then move on to other opportunities without a sustainability plan in place.

The process as noted in Figure 4.5 produces the third piece of the puzzle which is outputs. The outputs are the desired end of the process. The most obvious examples are excellence in customer satisfaction, quality, safety and the like. Each focus will have associated metrics and data to justify the goal attainment. Other outputs of the QMS may include standardization, efficiency and synergy. Synergy occurs when the parts of the QMS work together and produce more than the individual parts. Irrespectively, a win is a win and the outputs should be rewarded.

The final piece of the basic QMS structure is governance. Again, governance varies based on industry, organization type, scope and footprint. But, the key is for the governing body to provide direction, oversight and accountability. At the end of the day, the buck stops with top leadership. If the QMS is ineffective, then governance has a major role to play and should not be overlooked.

So, what's the takeaway from the QMS model structure discussion. One, a basic QMS should have at minimum four parts: inputs, process, outputs and governance. Two, the QMS process should identify and solve issues. Three, the outcomes should be validated, significant, recognized and rewarded. Lastly, governance and top leaders are ultimately responsible for the success or failure of the QMS.

MARKET QMS ROLL UP STRUCTURE

Figure 4.6 outlines a larger scale QMS model structure.

Again, the QMS model will depend upon the organization's size, scope, complexity and footprint. For this example, the organization has ten business units spread over a large geographic footprint. Each business unit is different in terms of scope, but they all are in the same business canvas.

The starting point of the figure is the system board. Here, there are multiple markets involved in various states. The system board oversees all governance activities of the entire enterprise as a whole. Thus, the system board is ultimately responsible for the organization's QMS outcomes. Simply put, the buck stops with this governance body.

Reporting to the system board is an enterprise quality executive council. This council is comprised of system level leaders who are experts in the quality arena. In healthcare, for example, this may entail both quality operational leaders and clinical leaders (i.e., physicians). The goal is for this council to act as a high-level filter for the QMS model. This council is responsible for ensuring technically the QMS is sound, structured properly and the process is effective via goal attainment. Any outcomes issues should be addressed here before going to the system board if possible.

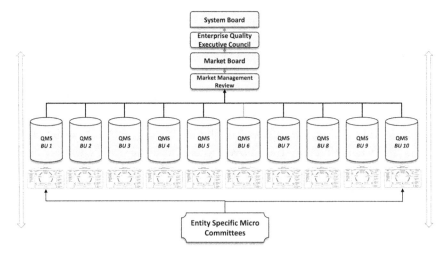

FIGURE 4.6
Market QMS roll up structure.

Next, each individual market in the enterprise portfolio has its own market board. This is a local governing body that focuses solely on the business units in the respective market. The goal would be for this group to ensure all outcomes tied to value are meeting goal, improving and in control. This board serves as local accountability and oversight for the market.

The next layer in the QMS structure for this example is management review. This phrase is derived from ISO 9001:205 directly. The management review group tends to be a small group of top executives in the market representing quality, operations, support services and talent management. They are expected to ensure the organization is aligned with the corporate structure, effective in meeting goals and improving.

Next, each business unit is represented in the figure. For this example, each unit has its own QMS model. The key is that each QMS is standardized and functions the same way. The difference is the nature of business and regulatory requirements. Each business unit is in a different business specialty and has varying requirements that govern the operating activities.

Reporting up to each QMS are various micro-level committees. The number of committees, their structure and focal points may vary from one business unit to the other. But, their main function is to identify, solve them and improve.

The goal with a market structure QMS model as outlined in the figure is to solve as many issues as possible at the lowest levels possible. Ideally, only high-level issues make up to the governance structure beyond the individual QMS models. If an organization has persistent issues tied to the value that are not solved in reasonable time periods, the governing body should be apprised and require correction. If not, both the QMS structure and governance are essentially ineffective. The adage of 'all pop, no fizz' will apply.

QMS PIPELINE

Another structural component of QMS leaders may value is the pipeline. See Figure 4.7 for details. This QMS pipeline is a one-page schematic of the QMS process. It's simply a horizontal and more detailed view of Figure 4.6. In the figure, the focal points are the five elements of excellence.

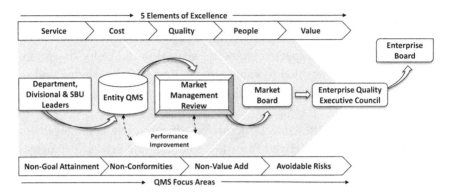

FIGURE 4.7
QMS pipeline.

Here, leaders and their organizations focus on service, cost, quality, people and value. These all have been described in detail throughout this book. Service applies to customer satisfaction regardless of industry. Cost may take on various meanings regardless of industry. Some organizations focus on per capita costs mainly.

Quality relates to the quality of services provided. In healthcare, for example, quality may focus on infection rates, safety, harm or mortality. People, as it relates to QMS, may include employee and leadership engagement, turnover, satisfaction, succession planning or many other attributes. Value is the overarching culmination of the other focal points mentioned.

The five elements of excellence are the start and main focal points for the QMS. Next, the QMS has a flow or process. It starts with the department or business unit leaders. These leaders are responsible for their value outcomes.

If issues persist in spite of improvement activities, then those items are escalated to the QMS leadership group. What QMS leaders cannot resolve is escalated to a higher group of market leaders (in this example) for resolution. The market management review group is comprised of a small group of senior leaders representing operations, technical arenas, talent management and support services.

Issues not resolved in management review are elevated to the market board for resolution. If the market board fails to solve critical issues tied to value, then the issues are sent to the executive quality council. These experts and thought leaders attempt to address the issues. If successful, improvements are sustained and continually improved. If improvements are lacking, the issues are escalated to the enterprise board or governing body.

The micro focal points or KPIs of focus for each step on the pipeline are listed at the bottom of the figure. Viable targets or focal points may include non-goal attainment for any value metrics, regulatory non-conformities, any non-value add and avoidable risks. The key is that the QMS focus areas should be specific, measurable and validated with data.

So, why is a QMS pipeline important to leaders and stakeholders? In short, one measure of success for a QMS model is if stakeholders can speak about it, understand the flow or reporting structure and resonate with its work. This tool is a simple one-page schematic leaders may use to ensure their QMS if effective.

QMS COMMITTEE DECISION TREE

One of the most common questions leaders vaguely familiar with QMS ask is 'How do we know what needs to go to QMS or other groups?' Figure 4.8 is a simple committee decision tree to help leaders understand where issues should flow.

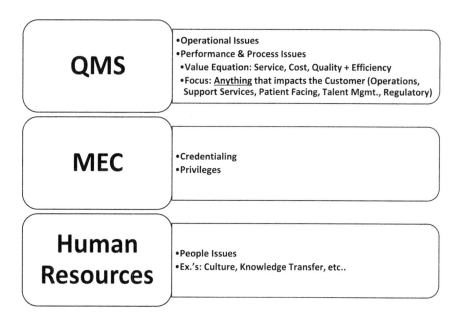

FIGURE 4.8
Committee decision tree.

The QMS, as previously noted, is a system comprised of people, structure and process. The makeup of this group may vary based on the organization's scope, size, complexity and structure.

Irrespectively, operational issues tied to the value equation should flow up to the QMS. These may include any non-goal attainment or risk tied to service, cost or quality as a starter. The QMS tends to focus on performance and process issues. In essence, the focus is anything that impact the customer. Far too often leaders silo QMS to only focus on quality. QMS is much more robust and far reaching than simple quality foci.

Another decision tree attribute, as used in the healthcare, is medical executive committee (MEC). In the healthcare arena, MEC is a group of physician leaders who focus on many provider topics such as credentialing, training and essentially the viability of medical providers to treat patients. Here, the issues with credentialing and privileges to provide healthcare services of providers is a good landing spot.

Finally, human resources (HR) is a common misperception that leaders should consider for the QMS committee structure. The HR committees also vary by industry and organization scope and in some organizations are separate from the QMS structure. But, the key is that HR or talent management tends to focus on hiring, discipline and firing functions. Compensation also plays a major role here as well. QMS leaders must ensure the applicable aspects of talent management are included in the QMS.

But, there aspects of talent management that may be appropriate for QMS. If turnover, for example, is a risk to meeting customer requirements then this may be a good topic for QMS leaders to entertain and address. Vacancy rates, employee engagement, succession planning and other topics also may quality or be a good fit for QMS. The key is for leaders to segment those talent management issues that are the highest risk to the customer and ensure they flow up through the QMS committee structure.

QMS TOPICS

Other often asked question by leaders relates to QMS topics. What do we need to focus on during QMS sessions? How much time should we spend on identified priorities? Again, the answers to these questions may vary based on the organization's size, scope, complexity, current operating environment and resourcing. There may also be regulatory requirements, for example in healthcare, that are required foci. Thus, leaders need to use insight and discretion when deciding what topics apply and time allotments for each.

A general rule of thumb can be viewed in Figure 4.9.

One common topic included in the QMS process is old business. Here, QMS leaders may focus on status updates on previous action items and results. This work may consume roughly 5% of the QMS agenda.

A major QMS topic area is inputs. Inputs may include items that are critical to quality, contribute to cost of poor quality, value metrics, data, regulatory non-conformities and any other improvement opportunities that are applicable. Leaders need to ensure that the proper inputs are focal points and addressed by the QMS model. Generally speaking, roughly 80% of the QMS agenda should be focused on the effectiveness of outcomes and action plans.

Another QMS topic worth noting is outputs. QMS time related to outputs may center around 10% of the agenda. Focus areas here center on KPI outcomes, changes to the QMS, resource needs and opportunities for improvement. Outputs are essentially a strong measure or indicator of the QMS model's success.

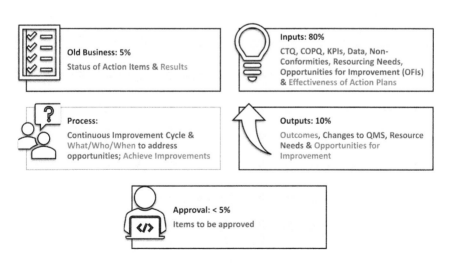

FIGURE 4.9
QMS topics.

The least focus for the QMS agenda is approval. Here, leaders may focus roughly 5% of the agenda on approving items. Much of the conversation is centered around regulatory requirements. Irrespectively, approval is a requirement and often needed function of QMS.

One last QMS hot topic is process. Here, QMS leaders ensure the continuous improvement cycle occurs. The process ensures all stakeholders know what is to be done, who owns what and when actions will be completed. The goal of the process is to filter opportunities to the top of organization's list.

VALUE PROPOSITION SAMPLE

The value proposition is a simple, but very critical structural aspect of QMS. Figure 4.10 is a very simple example of a value proposition statement. It simply outlines how the QMS model adds value to its stakeholders, customers and the organization. In the sample, items such as improvement, knowledge, excellence, strategy, safety, customer requirements, quality, value, team, innovation and efficiency all contribute to the QMS value proposition.

The sample value proposition is, 'Create Innovative Models and Concepts to Transform Healthcare Quality and Safety.' The key is for

Create Innovative Models and Concepts to Transform Healthcare Quality and Safety

FIGURE 4.10
Value proposition sample.

QMS leaders to state how the QMS provides value to its stakeholders. Each attribute of the value proposition needs to be specific, measurable and validated.

GUIDING THEMES

Guiding themes are a very important structural component worth noting. See Figure 4.11 for details.

There are many guiding themes that leaders may consider for the QMS model. These themes may include synergy, efficiency, evidence-based decisions, improvement, cultural alignment, value and the like. Irrespective of theme chosen, the QMS leaders need to select guiding themes that will

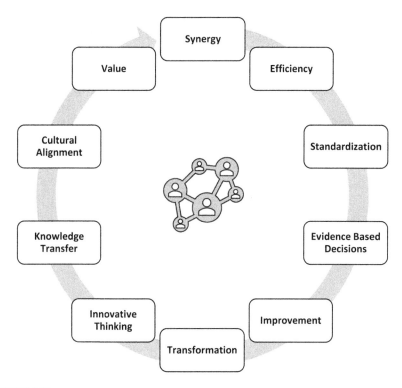

FIGURE 4.11
Guiding themes.

guide the future trajectory of the QMS model. Moreover, these themes should be aligned directly with organization's strategic direction.

Let's review some of the sample guiding themes. Synergy may be a good choice. This theme occurs when leaders, staff and teams work together and produce more together than apart. Efficiency occurs when organizations utilize minimal resources to achieve the desired end. Improvement is making the future state better than the current state.

These are just a few examples. The takeaway is the leaders must outline the road ahead, tollgates to be achieved and mechanisms for success. Each guiding theme should be correlated with goals, data and measurable outcomes.

STRATEGIC PILLARS

One final structural attribute for QMS leaders to consider is strategic pillars. These pillars are the foundation top leaders and those QMS leaders must align with the QMS structure. They also correlate directly to the value equation. As noted in Figure 4.12, sample pillars may include safety, efficiency, improvement, customer satisfaction and quality as examples.

The key here is for the organization's governing body to identify major focal points for the enterprise as a whole. Then, QMS leaders roll these

FIGURE 4.12
Strategic pillars.

pillars into the QMS infrastructure. The enterprise as a whole then develops tactical plans to be the best in the business in these arenas.

Step one is to identify and meet goals tied to each pillar. Step two is to improve organizational outcomes tied to each pillar. Step three to ensure strategic pillar outcomes are in control, stable and predictable via use of control charts. The ultimate test of a QMS model is structure, process and outcomes. These strategic pillars are structural paradigms needed to drive the desired outcomes.

NOTE

1. IISE, Lean Green Belt. 2016

5

The QMS Process

The purpose of the chapter is to outline the QMS process. A process is simply a series of steps that leads to a desired end. In our world today, everything involves a process to some level. Thus, QMS leaders must be process experts. Over the years, it's amazing how many leaders misperceive the QMS process as the 'meeting.'

Yes, meeting is a part of the process. But, it does not reflect the QMS process in its entirety. In the following discussion, leaders will learn how to leverage simple and effective tools to construct, assess and implement a viable QMS model. Without a good process, the QMS will not work.

Let's take a closer look.

QMS BUILDING PROCESS

Discovery

One of the initial steps to a viable QMS model is the building process. As noted in Figure 5.1, this process begins with discovery.

The discovery occurs when a leader assesses the organization's operating canvas to answer what is working, what is not working and what is missing as it relates to QMS. The first discovery phase is the risk assessment.

A risk assessment is exactly as it sounds. An assessment of the organization's current state risk. A risk is anything that can jeopardize success. In layman's terms, a risk is anything that will dissatisfy, harm or jeopardize the organization, its stakeholders and customers. But, how will leaders know their risks if they don't measure? In short, they won't.

 DOI: 10.4324/9781003485131-5

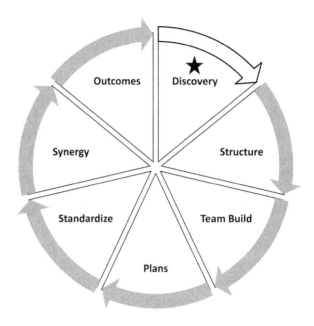

 Starting Point

FIGURE 5.1
QMS building process.

In simplest of terms, leaders should map out the current state. This includes what metrics are not meeting goal, not improving or out of control. This will be discussed more in the next chapter. Also, the current state assessment includes an overview of any waste. In the lean world, waste can include delays, errors, reworks, non-utilized talent, overproducing more than the customer is willing to pay for and the like. [1] Any waste is a high-risk proposition.

A common tool leaders may use during the discovery process is a voice of the customer survey. Here, QMS leaders focus on internal customers. Simply put, anyone involved with or affected by the QMS model is surveyed blindly for objective and honest feedback. The goal is to capture feedback and insight as to what stakeholders feel or perceive are the strengths, weaknesses and opportunities of QMS. A simple survey if leveraged properly can provide great insight as to the QMS process, its successes and weak spots.

Structure Assessment

Once the discovery phase is complete, QMS leaders focus on the structure. We have already touched on this in previous chapters. But, the theme is for leaders to review the current state structure and identify what is working as well as what is missing. Common foci include the organizational chart and functional chart. Here, leaders review the current organizational chart to understand where QMS fits, who it reports to, who is responsible for the QMS and the like. The goal is to ensure the QMS has adequate leadership and sponsorship from senior leaders.

The functional chart is similar, but focuses mainly on the grouping of various functions. For example, is the QMS paired with a performance improvement function? If so, great. If not, how will the QMS improve its outcomes? If performance improvement is not collated within or adjacent to the QMS structure, then there is a good chance the process will not work.

Another aspect of the process involves a review and alignment of roles and responsibilities. Do QMS leaders understand their role in the QMS? Have these roles been outlined in the QMS charter? Have leaders agreed to resume these responsibilities? If not, the process may fail.

There are other structural aspects of the QMS process we will discuss later.

Team Building

Once leaders develop a better understanding of the current state via discovery, they begin team building. Here, QMS leaders begin the relationship management process to drive outcomes. Relationship management is often erroneously correlated with playing politics. In reality, managing relationships begins with establishing trust.

Trust is not whether someone likes or prefers another person. Formally, trust occurs when several conditions are met. One, everyone contributes to success. People need to see where they fit in the QMS structure and how they help the team succeed.

Two, everyone focuses on excellence. Here, all stakeholders must commit to excellent work, outcomes and teamwork. Three, trust is dependent upon a safe place to succeed and fail. Along the journey, all leaders will experience both success and failure. Failure is not a death sentence (professionally speaking). Often, failures are just a set up for the next success. Irrespectively, trust is required for team building to succeed.

During team building, QMS leaders may leverage feedback sessions. This may include surveys or in person interaction where QMS leaders engage stakeholders to better understand their preferences, needs, fears and the like. The better leaders understand their stakeholders, the greater the chance of success in meeting their expectations.

The end goal of team building is to create synergies where QMS accomplishes more together with all stakeholders than working in silos. When synergy is present, leaders often find the QMS to function more efficiently and produce better outcomes. In contrast, silos breed inefficiency and non-performance.

Plans

Planning is one of the most important aspects of the QMS process. The biggest pitfall leaders can succumb to is implementing a QMS without a well-defined, measurable and socialized plan. The first consideration for leaders is a first 100-day plan. What will the QMS and its leaders accomplish in the first 100 days? Can you summarize this in one slide with the main bullet points? If so, great. If not, there is a good chance stakeholders, governance and leaders may not understand the QMS process or its destination. Common attributes of the 100-day plan may include the assessment, gap analysis, road map, five-year plan and many other attributes.

Planning for QMS also involves several other plans such as knowledge, change, improvement, readiness, communication and training. The knowledge plans will depend upon the organization's needs and resources. In simplest of terms, the knowledge plan may include several foci: succession planning, cross training, coaching, mentoring, a knowledge management system and others. The key is for the QMS to ensure knowledge is being shared both inside the enterprise and externally. The knowledge plan should include measurable metrics, goals and improvement.

The next plan should evolve around change. Since change is the new normal, leaders must plan for it. With change comes risk. Thus, QMS leader must assess, analyze and mitigate risks to the QMS. The change plan can simply entail a list of the significant changes that impacted the QMS in the last year. Also, leaders will need to include expected changes forthcoming. Each change should be risk assessed as to the level of actual or expected risk to the QMS and organizational as a whole. Once prioritized, the leaders must ensure a plan is in place to implement each change in the most controlled and least disrupting way possible.

Another common plan addressed during the QMS process relates to improvement. Common considerations may include the following:

- What are the QMS improvement targets?
- Does each target have available and accurate data?
- Are the targets aligned with the organization's strategy?
- Does the QMS or the overarching organization have adequate improvement resources to assist the QMS process?
- Have these resources been formally trained in recognized methodologies?
- Do the improvers have the resources they need to succeed?
- Does the organization have a training plan for the future?
- If improvement leaders leave the organization or get reassigned to another role, is there a pipeline to ensure gaps will not occur?
- How will improvements be shared to internal stakeholders and externally?
- How will wins with improvement teams be validated?
- How will improvement teams be rewarded and celebrated?

These are just a few considerations for improvement plans. The takeaway is that a good QMS process will consider these attributes.

The readiness plan is also a part of the QMS process. This pertains mainly to regulatory requirements. But, the QMS leaders will need to ensure that the organization and QMS stakeholders understand and are accountable to regulatory requirements that impact the QMS. Also, leaders must ensure readiness plans include audit teams of some fashion. Audit teams are extremely beneficial in ensuring the organization is ready or compliant at all times. These plans may include an operating calendar for audits, team distributions to ensure all aspects of the enterprise are covered and represented, and a process so audit outcomes flow through the QMS process.

Another plan that is directly tied to the QMS process is communication. How will the QMS communicate to its stakeholders? What mode of communication will work best and be best received? What is the frequency of communication? Who will own the communication process? Who will be responsible for responding to inquires or requests? There are many considerations for a communication plan tied to the QMS. But, leaders must ensure one exists, it's effective and measurable. Otherwise, what stakeholders don't know will hamper the QMS success.

Finally, QMS leaders must include a training plan in the QMS process. Training may include regulatory updates, methodologies and the like. The targets will include front-line staff up to the governing body. The key is to ensure the QMS adds value to all its stakeholders by ensuring they are trained, equipped for success and prepared to help the QMS thrive.

Standardization

Once plans are developed and approved, the QMS process focuses on standardizing as much as it can where it makes sense. Again, standardization will depend upon the organization's culture, resource base and current agenda. Common tactics to standardize include but are not limited to agendas, report out slides, A3s, meeting minutes, improvement outcomes, KPIs, data visual display and the like. The key is for leaders to standardize every aspect of the QMS process where it makes sense. Otherwise, variation and waste will impede the QMS from reaching its full potential.

Synergy

The next step in the QMS building process is synergy. We have discussed this previously. So, for simplicity sake let's keep it simple. QMS leaders must ensure synergy exists where the various parts of the QMS work together, produce more as a whole and avoid silos. This will ensure the QMS process is effective, efficient and high performing.

Outcomes

The final aspect of the QMS building process is outcomes. Outcomes commonly focus on goal attainment for predetermined metrics. There are many outcomes or measures of success we will discuss in the next chapter. But, leaders must ensure the goals established in the plans around readiness, compliance, improvement, knowledge sharing and the like are achieved. Once goals are attained, the QMS should look to improve upon those wins. This is the spirit of continuous improvement and will ensure long-term QMS viability.

QMS TEMPLATE STRUCTURE

As noted in Figure 5.2, a QMS template structure is very important to its process.

In simplest of forms, QMS needs several basic attributes for the process to be effective. First, leaders should assemble a simple, clear and effective agenda. In simplest of terms, the agenda should be dated and include basics such as what is to be covered, who owns it, next steps for action items and who owns the deliverables.

Also, QMS leaders should consider utilizing meeting minutes. Some organizations will be required to take minutes due to regulatory requirements. Irrespectively, the minutes also should be simple and outline the basics of the QMS meeting conversations. What was discussed, deliverables coming due and who owns what at minimum. Here, the simpler the better.

QMS leaders may also consider a consent agenda. In simplest of terms the consent agenda is a summary of what is working. This may include data or other information meeting goal for example. Instead of spending QMS meeting time focus heavily on what is working, this material may be shared in a consent agenda prior to the meeting with stakeholders so the meeting time can focus on opportunities for improvement.

The KPI template is also a useful tool we will discuss later. In essence, QMS leaders must ensure the QMS process is template driven for organization and uniformity. This template is a simple presentation tool QMS leaders will use to capture and display their metrics data. The simpler the better.

Some QMS leaders leverage an A3. We will also cover this more later. But the key is for leaders to capture as much information as possible on

- Agenda
- Meeting Minutes
- Consent Agenda
  - Summary of *'What is Working'*; KPI Template showcase
- KPI Template
  - Run chart, control chart, notes
- QMS A3
- A3 Root Cause Summary
- Performance Improvement Detailed Showcase
  - All projects detail-see spreadsheet (PI Program Outcomes Showcase)
  - Publications of 'Wins'

FIGURE 5.2
QMS template structure.

their metrics in one slide. The goal is for QMS stakeholders to see visually at minimum the problem, the goal, a graph with performance to goal and a list of actions to address improvement opportunities.

An A3 root cause summary is also helpful. This tool allows QMS leaders to attach more information to each A3 template as it relates to root causes and drivers of issues. The root cause summary also provides visual display of what-who-when. In short, what is to be done, who owns it and when will it be completed?

QMS leaders should also consider a performance improvement detailed showcase. This showcase includes details of each project or initiative that stem from the QMS process. If asked for a list of QMS initiatives by senior leader, what would you present? Would you have to reinvent the wheel or create something on the fly? Or could you easily share a well thought out showcase detailing the project, its scope, current status and outcomes to date?

QMS MEETING TEMPLATE

Figure 5.3 outlines a very simple meeting template QMS leaders may find helpful. For each KPI to be reviewed in QMS, the template includes sections for a run chart, a control chart and notes that describe the data

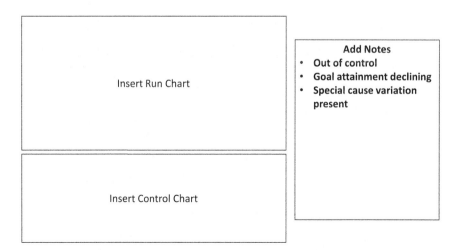

FIGURE 5.3
QMS meeting template.

outcomes noted in the charts. We will discuss both run and control charts in the next chapter. But, this simple schematic clearly outlines outcomes, lack thereof and control of metrics. QMS leaders must realize that not all QMS stakeholders will be context experts. Often, less is more and simplicity speaks volumes to novice QMS stakeholders.

Figure 5.4 is a mock and complete version of Figure 5.3. Here, the run chart is displayed in the top box. The run chart is simply a line graph with data points, an average line and goal line. The key is for stakeholders to see improvements or lack thereof based on the average line's position to goal. In this example, the metric is improving to goal over the three-year period. But, it's still not meeting goal.

The control chart is positioned below the run chart. It's a simple schematic of the same data in the run chart with control limits. It will take more understanding of statistical process control for stakeholders to understand and leverage the value of control charts. In the example, the data is out of control. Thus, special cause variation is present. This means leaders need to take note as special circumstances are present.

Irrespectively, this tool is a simple visual display tool QMS leaders may find of value for their metrics and presentations in QMS.

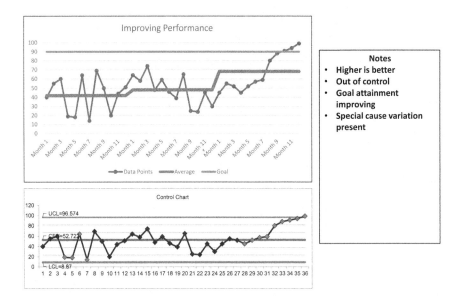

FIGURE 5.4
QMS meeting sample template.

QMS A3 SCOPING FORM

Figure 5.5 is a tool that QMS leaders may find valuable. In simplest of terms, the A3 scoping form includes a section for the problem and goal statements. Also, on the top right of the figure it outlines the responsible leader, the department and date. Focus areas of the presentation are also a good focal point to note. As noted, there is a placeholder for the KPI graph as noted in the previous example. Then, leaders can list the root causes of non-performance. Finally, at the bottom right of the figure is a what-who-when chart for each root cause.

The takeaway is for leaders to visually display their performance outcomes in one document.

QMS A3 ROOT CAUSE DETAIL SUMMARY

The root cause summary often serves as an addendum to the template in Figure 5.6. Here, the leaders list the root causes for each KPI. Each KPI will outline drivers or micro root causes and what is to be done for correction along with who owns it. Some leaders use this information for consent agendas, presentations for QMS sessions and detailed summary reference material for regulatory surveys. If you find value in it, then it's a good tool for visually displaying more detail when needed.

QMS MEETING TEMPLATE INSTRUCTIONS

Figure 5.7 is a template for QMS leaders to facilitate their meetings. This also is a good schematic that QMS leaders may want to consider for stakeholder training sessions. The goal is to include a schematic on the right-hand side of the matrix. This will provide stakeholders with a simple overview of the reporting structure up through QMS to the governing body.

On the right side of the template are simple instructions for QMS leaders to prepare their QMS presentations for the sessions. The goal is for leaders to list what is expected of each stakeholder accompanied with a template whether it be A3 or other template. One of the biggest pitfalls QMS leaders may experience is expecting one thing from stakeholders and not adequately outlining those expectations in or with templates.

Responsible Leader: Dept.(s):   Date:

Focus Area (Circle One):   Service   Cost   Quality   People   Value

INSERT KPI GRAPH
At least 12-24 Months of Data
Include: Goal line, Current KPI trend line & Avg KPI Goal Attainment line

Root Cause	What (Action Plan)	Who (Owns It)	When (To be Completed)

Problem Statement | *Add information*

Goal Statement | *Add information*

Root Cause List:
- *Add info*
- *Add info*
- *Add info*
- *Add info*
- *Add info*

QMS Meeting Date	KPI (s)	Goal	Current Score	Gap (%)

FIGURE 5.5
QMS A3 Scoping form.

	Responsible Leader: John Doe	Entity/Dept.(s): 'A'		Date:
	Focus Area (Circle One):	Service Cost Quality People Value		

(1) Problem Statement: *Patient satisfaction is 35th percentile in department 'A'*

(2)

Root Cause Road Map	Drivers (Reason(s) for Root Cause)	What (Action Plan for Drivers)	Who (Owns It)	When (Completed)	Status • Complete • In Progress • Past Due
Wait Times	• Transport • Low staffing on weekends • Registration process delays	• Add additional transport staff M-F • Increase weekend staff Jan 1st • Green Belt project begins Jan 1st	• John Doe • Jane Doe • Jane Doe	• 1/1/19 • 1/15/19 • 1/15/19	• Complete • In Progress • In Progress
Pain Medication Delays	• Low staffing at night • Medication stock out • MD Signatures	• Request FTE for weekends • Green Belt project in Pharmacy • Address in MEC	• Jane Doe • Jane Doe • John Doe	• 1/1/19	• Past Due
Room Cleanliness		• Process Mapping	• John Doe	• 1/1/19	
Provider Rounding Delays		• Driver Diagram	• Jane Doe	• 2/1/19	
Test result delays		• RCA, Fishbone	• John Doe	• 2/1/19	
Add info					
Add info					
Add info					

FIGURE 5.6

Root cause detail summary.

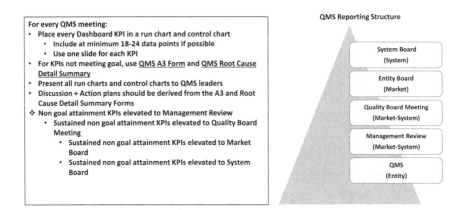

QMS Reporting Structure

For every QMS meeting:
- Place every Dashboard KPI in a run chart and control chart
  - Include at minimum 18-24 data points if possible
  - Use one slide for each KPI
- For KPIs not meeting goal, use <u>QMS A3 Form</u> and <u>QMS Root Cause Detail Summary</u>
- Present all run charts and control charts to QMS leaders
- Discussion + Action plans should be derived from the A3 and Root Cause Detail Summary Forms
- ❖ Non goal attainment KPIs elevated to Management Review
  - Sustained non goal attainment KPIs elevated to Quality Board Meeting
    - Sustained non goal attainment KPIs elevated to Market Board
    - Sustained non goal attainment KPIs elevated to System Board

System Board (System)

Entity Board (Market)

Quality Board Meeting (Market-System)

Management Review (Market-System)

QMS (Entity)

FIGURE 5.7
QMS meeting template instructions.

REQUIRED QMS ATTENDEES TEMPLATE

Figure 5.8 is a template or showcase for leaders to outline who should attend a QMS session. There are specific regulatory requirements that may affect or dictate this list. The figure is just an example of one way to showcase the attendees for a multi-facility organization.

The key is for the template to outline leadership categories for required attendees. Also, for each business unit QMS leaders will need to list the exact title of each leader type who must attend. Irrespective of industry or organizational need, one of the most common questions top leaders ask is who has to attend QMS sessions. Figure 5.8 is a simple outline that QMS leaders may find of value. But, the content will need to be tailored to the specific organization's operating canvas.

GOVERNANCE ATTENDEES TEMPLATE

As noted previously, governance is an organizationally driven process. Thus, leaders will need to adapt their attendees templates based on the organization's need, structure, scope and complexity.

Figure 5.9 outlines a higher-level management review model. The difference between Figures 5.8 and 5.9 is that Figure 5.9 focuses on high-level

Required Attendees	BU 1	BU 2	BU 3	BU 4	BU 5
Senior Leadership	• COO • CNO/VP • CHRO	• CEO • COO	• CEO • COO	• CAO-VP • AVP	• CEO • Director(s)
Medical Staff	• CMO • Medical Director(s) • AVP Medical Affairs	• CMO	• CMO	• CMO	• CMO
Nursing	• VP/AVP • Director(s) Ad Hoc	• CNO	• CNO	• CNO	• CNO
Quality/Risk Management *(Management Representative)*	• AVP • Director • Managers Ad Hoc	• Director • Manager	• Director • Manager	• Director • Manager	• Director • Manager
Physical Environment/Safety	• VP • AVP/Director • Manager Ad Hoc	• Director • Manager	• Director • Manager	• Director • Manager	• Director • Manager
Pharmacy Services	• AVP • Director • Manager Ad Hoc	• Director • Manager	• Director • Manager	• Director • Manager	• Director • Manager
Ancillary Services *(Ex.'s-HR; Accreditation; Supply Chain, Patient Experience, IS, Nutrition Services, EVS, etc.....)*	• VP • AVP • Director	• Director • Manager	• Director • Manager	• Director • Manager	• Director • Manager

FIGURE 5.8
Required QMS attendees.

System Wide Focus Areas	Required Attendees	Ad Hoc Attendees

Clinical/Quality	• EVP Clinical
	• CMO
	• Chief Quality Officer
	• CNE/CNO
		• Entity Leaders
		  • CEO
		  • CAO
		  • CMO
		  • CNO
		  • COO
		• Others TBD
		  • Divisional Leaders

Operations	• EVP Operations • System COO	
Ancillary Services (Ex.'s-HR; Accreditation; Supply Chain, Patient Experience, IS, Nutrition Services, EVS, etc.....)	• EVP Operations • System COO	
People (Talent Management)	• CHRO	
Service (Patient Experience)	• EVP Operations • System COO	
Performance Improvement	• Chief Results Officer • Chief Outcomes Officer • System Black Belt • AVP PMO Ad Hoc	
Support	• Accreditation • Management Representative	

FIGURE 5.9
Required management review attendees.

leadership meetings that is the direct report group up to the QMS in some organizational types. The key is for leaders to display in one slide the focus areas needed in the room, what leadership titles are associated with each focus area and ad hoc attendees.

The reality is that time is very valuable and expensive. Top leaders will attempt to free up their time so they can invest in better options elsewhere. If QMS leaders are asked who needs to be in the room for higher-level leaders QMS related meetings, a simple one-page schematic will be greatly beneficial to simplify the conversation. The figure is just a simple example that leaders may find value in.

QMS SAMPLE TOPICS

Over the years its unimaginable how much time leaders spend on discussing meeting topics. Figure 5.10 is a simple schematic QMS leaders may find beneficial in knowing what topics QMS leaders should focus on. The key is for leaders to craft the list and schematic to their organization's need. On the left side of the template, leaders would list the areas that are required to report out in the QMS session. On the right, leaders list the focal points or KPIs needed for discussion in the meetings.

The key is to ensure the QMS process is as efficient as possible. The goal is for leaders to cover required elements, but not waste time focusing on items that are not of value. At the end of the day, QMS leaders may need a one-page schematic that outlines this information.

GOVERNANCE MEETING OPERATING STRUCTURE TEMPLATE

Figure 5.11 is a template QMS leaders may find helpful for high-level governance activities. This tool is also a simple one-pager that outlines the meeting, frequency, focus area and attendees. Again, the purpose is for QMS leaders to have a one-pager they can present at moment's notice that outlines the governance activity, who attends and focus areas. This too is a hot topic discussion area amongst leaders.

Irrespectively, QMS leaders will need to craft the template to their organization's scope, complexity and operating structure.

Area	Topic
Facilities Management	• Work order TATs; Critical Events (Power outages, leaks/floods, etc....); Re-work work orders
EVS	• Response times; TATs
Nutrition Services	• Response times; TATs; accuracy of orders; food quality
Accreditation	• Non-conformities; critical non-conformities; Corrective Actions
Pharmacy	• Stock out rates; response times; error rates; delays
Human Resources	• Onboarding time-vacant roles; vacancy rates; turnover rates; succession planning
Clinical Quality	• Quality metrics
Information Services	• Call Center request trends; TATs
Supply Chain	• Stock outs; expired supplies; delivery times; Error rates-delivering wrong items
Patient Experience	• Areas meeting vs not meeting goals
Internal Voice of Customer Survey Outcomes	• Stakeholder satisfaction
Approvals	• Policies and process changes

FIGURE 5.10
QMS sample topics.

Meeting	Frequency	Focus Area(s)	Attendees
QMS (Entity)	Monthly	• Entity Centric • Approvals • Performance Opportunities	• Entity Leaders
Management Review (Market)	Monthly	• Entity/Market Centric • Approvals • Performance Opportunities • Synergy, Standardization, Effectiveness, Efficiency, Outcomes	• Market Leaders
Market Board (Market)	Monthly	• Market Centric • Approvals • Performance Opportunities • Synergy, Standardization, Effectiveness, Efficiency, Outcomes	• Market Board + • Market Leaders
Enterprise Quality Executive Council	Monthly	• Market/Enterprise Centric • Approvals • Performance Opportunities • Synergy, Standardization, Effectiveness, Efficiency, Outcomes	• Enterprise Quality Senior Leaders
Enterprise Board	Monthly	• Enterprise Centric	• Enterprise Board + • Enterprise Leaders

FIGURE 5.11
Governance meeting operating structure.

GOVERNANCE MEETING OPERATING CALENDAR TEMPLATE

Figure 5.12 is a simple template for an annual high-level view of the governance operating calendar. QMS leaders simply list the meeting categories that occur throughout the year. Then, notate in which months each governance group meets. This will help the QMS process flow smoothly and ensure required elements of regulatory functions are not lost in translation. This type of template is greatly beneficial in the planning phase of the QMS process.

As noted previously, leaders will need to craft a template that applies to their specific organizational type.

REPORT OUT SHOWCASE TEMPLATE

The report out showcase is a simple tool QMS leaders may find of value as well. In Figure 5.13, it's a simple assessment tool of how many macro KPIs are not meeting goal. Column 1 represents the entity or business unit dependent upon how the organization is structured. The second column is the focus area or KPI. The next two columns outline the number of initiatives or KPIs not meeting goal along with the responsible leader.

The key is for leaders, particularly in organizations with large geographic footprints, to understand globally how well or poor each business unit or QMS model is performing. This will ensure adequate improvement resources are assigned to the highest risk areas.

Either way, QMS leaders will need to craft the template to meet their organization's structure, needs and operating calendar.

REPORT OUT CALENDAR TEMPLATE

Figure 5.14 is a calendar for report out to QMS. This is a more micro view of the initiatives. In the first column, leaders list the focus areas for each QMS for the year. Then, score which months those focus areas will report to the leaders. The key is that there may be regulatory requirements that influence this calendar. But, it's a good rule of thumb for QMS leaders to incorporate this level of detail in their plans so the QMS process is both efficient and effective.

Meeting	Jan	Feb	Mar	Apr	May	Jun	July	Aug	Sep	Oct	Nov	Dec
QMS (Entity)	X		X		X		X		X		X	
Management Review (Market)		X		X		X		X		X		X
Market Board (Market)	X			X			X			X		
Enterprise Quality Executive Council	X	X	X	X	X	X	X	X	X	X	X	X
System Board		X		X		X		X		X		X

FIGURE 5.12

Governance meeting operating calendar.

Entity	Focus	# of Initiatives (Non-Goal Attainment)	Executive Sponsor
Entity 1	• Quality Scores • Patient Satisfaction	• 5 • 10	• John Doe • Jane Doe
Entity 2	• Quality Scores • Patient Satisfaction	• 2 • 2	• John Doe • Jane Doe
Entity 3	• Quality Scores • Patient Satisfaction	• 2 • 2	• John Doe • Jane Doe
Entity 4	• Quality Scores • Patient Satisfaction	• 3 • 3	• John Doe • Jane Doe
Entity 5	• Quality Scores • Patient Satisfaction	• 1 • 1	• John Doe • Jane Doe
Total		31	

FIGURE 5.13
Report out: Current initiatives 'Show case'.

Focus Area	Jan	Feb	Mar	Apr	May	Jun	July	Aug	Sep	Oct	Nov	Dec
Quality Scores • Quality Scores	X		X		X		X		X		X	
Service • Customer Satisfaction		X		X		X		X		X		X
Operations • Costs	X			X			X			X		
People • Vacancies, Turnover, Engagement, Onboarding	X	X	X	X	X	X	X	X	X	X	X	X
Support Services		X		X		X		X		X		X
Regulatory	X			X			X			X		
Approvals • Ad Hoc	X	X	X	X	X	X	X	X	X	X	X	X

FIGURE 5.14
Report out: 'Calendar-focus areas'.

REPORT OUT CURRENT INITIATIVES SHOWCASE TEMPLATE

Figure 5.15 outlines a simple template for specific projects or initiative involving the QMS. This was discussed briefly previously. Here, leaders list each project. These projects may also be listed on the A3 root cause

Initiative	Entity/ Dept.	Focus/Dept. (Problem?)	Start Date	Level (BB/GB/RCA/Quick Win)	Phase DMA	Phase Improve	Phase Control	Status	Completion Date
Project 1 *Name of Project*	BU 1	Delays in department 'x'	1-1-21	Quick Win	X			IP	
Project 2 *Name of Project*	BU 2	Errors in department 'Y'	1-2-21	RCA			X	C	1/10/2021
Project 3 *Name of Project*	BU 3	Overproduction in department 'Z'	1-2-21	Green Belt		X		CR	
Project 4 *Name of Project*									
Project 5 *Name of Project*									
Project 6 *Name of Project*									
Project 7 *Name of Project*									
Project 8 *Name of Project*									
Project 9 *Name of Project*									

CR=Critical (High Priority)
IP=In Progress (Work-to-Do)
C=Complete

RCA = Root Cause Analysis
DMA = Define, Measure & Analyze

FIGURE 5.15

Report out: Current initiatives 'Show case'.

summary template as well. The key is for QMS leaders to capture all the initiatives, where they are taking place, start date, status and completion date.

The larger the scope of the QMS, generally speaking, the larger the number of initiatives. These initiatives or projects are essentially tied back to non-performing KPIs or other root causes. Some projects may be a simple root cause analysis. Other activity may include Lean or Six Sigma projects. Irrespective of the technique used, QMS leaders will need to track projects and display them in a showcase.

QMS COMMUNICATION SCHEDULE TEMPLATE

Figure 5.16 is a sample QMS communication schedule. The key for this tool is to answer who needs QMS communication, who will be responsible for the communication, the frequency, format and type of communication. This information is greatly important during the communication planning process for QMS.

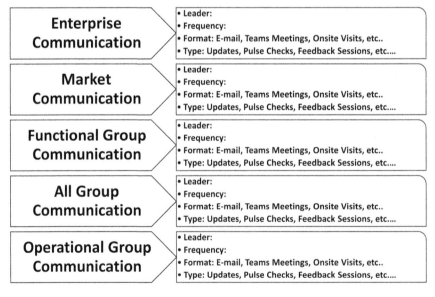

FIGURE 5.16
QMS communication schedule.

Irrespective of the format chosen, QMS leaders need to know who their stakeholders are and what communication is applicable to each group. As noted in the example, there is communication to QMS stakeholders ranging from enterprise leaders to operational groups. The goal is for leaders to understand their constituents and leverage communication that is relevant to the desired end user.

This tool as well will need to be crafted to the organization's needs, scope and operating canvas.

COMMUNICATION FRAMEWORK TEMPLATE

The communication framework template in Figure 5.17 is a simple tool that QMS leaders can leverage. The purpose of the template is to capture a micro level view of QMS communications. Details may include the responsible leader, topic, scope, target audience, method and frequency. This tool will ensure QMS leaders are aligned with the needed communication over the course of the year.

It's important for a QMS leader to understand, track and visually display communication activities so the QMS process is effective and efficient. This too will enhance visibility, trust and ease of implementing the QMS process.

QMS FIVE-YEAR PLAN TEMPLATE

One of the core elements of a QMS process is the five-year plan. QMS leaders need to ensure the QMS vision aligns with the organization's future trajectory. This template begins with focus areas. For the sample in Figure 5.18, the focus areas include structure, process, knowledge sharing, visual display of data, regulatory deficiencies and standardization.

Here, the QMS leaders have outlined a five-year plan for each focus area. For the QMS structure, year 1 is slated for the assessment. The goal is for QMS leaders to assess the QMS, identify gaps and begin planning to fill gaps. Year 2 focuses on inputs and process. Leaders would intend to

Responsible Leader	Topic	Scope	Target Audience	Method	Frequency
John Doe	Updates	Market Wide	Leaders	In Person	Monthly
Jane Doe	Pulse Checks	Business Unit 1	All Staff	E-mail	Monthly
Jack Doe	Feedback Sessions	Business Units 3 & 4	Leaders and Staff	Social Media Post	Quarterly

FIGURE 5.17
Communication framework.

QMS 5 Year Plan

Focus Area	Year 1	Year 2	Year 3	Year 4	Year 5
Structure	• Assessment	• Inputs + Process	• Outcomes	• Governance	• Integrated Structure
Process	• Discovery	• Scope high priority items	• Implement improvement program	• Realize improvement outcomes	• Sustain improvement outcomes
Knowledge Sharing	• Publish 1 Article	• Publish 1 Article	• Publish 1 Article	• Publish 1 Article	• Publish 1 Article
Data Visual Display	• Introduce Run Charts	• Implement Run Charts	• Introduce Control Charts	• Implement Control Charts	• Poster Boards in all work areas
Regulatory Deficiencies	• Discovery	• Target high risk areas	• Measurable reductions	• Target medium risk areas	• Target low risk areas
Standardization	• Data	• Meeting agendas & A3s	• Presentation slides	• Structures	• Process

FIGURE 5.18
QMS Five year plan.

ensure all QMS inputs are present and applicable as needed. Also, leaders would ensure in this year that the process is effective, efficient and aligned with the QMS model. Years 3 through 5 would focus on outcomes, governance and integrating the structure. This is just one example in the template.

QMS leaders can easily map out their main strategic focus areas over a five-year increment. This too will need to be tailored to the organization's size, scope, strategic direction and operating fabric. But, the main takeaway is to ensure the QMS five-year plan is aligned with the organization's strategic plan.

NOTE

1. IISE, Lean Green Belt. 2016

6

Measuring QMS Success

One of the most important aspects of any quality management system (QMS) model is success? But, how will leaders know if the QMS is successful without measurement? Simply put, they won't. Over the years it's shocking how many leaders can't define success for their QMS model.

Some leaders view a successful QMS by the attendance at meetings. Others view their QMS as successful if the attendees are engaged and participate in good conversation. Another common thread perception of QMS success leaders often succumb to is standardization. The adage is "Were successful with QMS because we do it the same at all our facilities." But, what if QMS is ineffective? Does standardization really matter at the point? Arguably, not.

There are several measures of success leaders must entertain when designing and assessing their QMS structure. Let's start with structure.

STRUCTURE

A QMS structure is the starting point when designing a high-performing QMS. But, what constitutes a good or successful structure?

1. Does the QMS structure have at least four parts: inputs, process, outputs and governance or oversight? If so, this is a good start to success.

DOI: 10.4324/9781003485131-6

2. Do inputs include attributes such as people, knowledge, data, regulatory requirements, improvement resources, methodology and many others? If so, this is a good sign of a successful QMS.

3. Is the QMS process cyclical with a focus on continuous improvement? Does the process act as a filter for risks to the customer such as non-goal attainment, regulatory non-conformities, waste and the like? Does the process identify customer risks and solve them? Does the process continually improve wins in this arena? If so, this is a component of a viable or successful QMS.

4. Are the outputs tied to the organization's strategic priorities such as excellence in quality, service, value and the like? Do the outputs include creating synergy, standardization and efficiency? If so, these are signs of success.

5. Is governance a staple of the QMS model? If so, then the QMS is primed for success.

6. Can leaders and stakeholders speak fluently about the QMS structure and how their business fits or relates to it? If so, this too is a success factor of QMS.

7. Is the QMS structure scalable or will it work only for specific business unit types? The key is that scalability is better than a silo approach for long-term viability, synergy and efficiency.

8. Can leaders display the QMS model on one slide? If so, this contributes to viability of the QMS model and its adoption by stakeholders.

9. Does the model focus on technical, operations, support services, regulatory and talent management or just mainly on technical aspects of the business model? QMS models that focus on all attributes have a better chance of success.

10. Is QMS standardized for all entities or business units as it relates to agendas, meeting minutes, slides, structure, leadership representation, A3s, etc.? If so, the probability of success is increased.

11. Are performance improvement resources assigned to and available to support leaders at all facilities or business units with non-performing outcomes? Without improvement resources, leaders will struggle to improve. Thus, the QMS may be marginally successful at best.

PROCESS

The QMS process is a very important measure of success. Let's review a few considerations leader's should entertain.

1. Does the QMS process include a continual discovery process where leaders constantly scan the organization's operating canvas for risks, non-goal attainment, regulatory deficiencies and the like? If so, the process is primed or success.
2. Does the QMS process involve planning? Are leaders including attributes into their QMS plans related to communication, training, knowledge sharing, improvement and current state readiness? If so, the process is successful.
3. Does the process utilize minimal resources to achieve the desired outcomes of the QMS? Simply stated, is the process efficient? If so, this is also a sign of success.
4. Does the QMS process include stakeholder feedback? Are stakeholders regularly surveyed as to their perception of the QMS, its efficiency, its effectiveness, etc.? Is so, the process is primed for success.
5. Does the QMS process champion standardization across all business units? If so, this is a sign of success.

GOVERNANCE MODEL

The governance model is ultimately responsible for the success or failure of the QMS. Thus, it must be measured and successful. Here are a few considerations for leaders to entertain as these pertain to success factors.

1. Is the current governance structure effective? Is there objective evidence in the form of value metrics goal attainment or improvements for example? If so, then this is a good sign of success.
2. Can leaders and stakeholders speak about the governance structure, its function and how they interact or relate to it? If so, the governance model is successful.

3. Is the governance structure displayed in one slide is sufficient for leaders and other stakeholders to refer? If the answer is yes, then this is a sign of success.

4. Is the structure what is needed for today's operating reality? Simply put, is the governance structure aligned with the organization's strategic direction, vision and true north? If so, this is a sign of success.

OUTCOMES

One of the most obvious and widely recognized measures of success for QMS is outcomes. QMS outcomes may refer to goal attainment, improvements and control of KPI outcomes. The KPIs of focus may include, but not be limited to safety, quality, cost, value, customer satisfaction, waste reduction, efficiency and the like. Regardless of foci, outcomes must be specific, measurable, significant and sustained for long term. But, are there other outcome considerations that may constitute success? Let's see.

Data Display

1. Is the right data being measured? If the QMS measures the right data to meet and exceed customer requirements, then this is a sign of success. The question to be answered is what's being measured and what needs to be measured?

2. Do templates exist for data display and are they being used by all stakeholders? At minimum, are run charts being utilized for each KPI? If so, can leaders and stakeholders access the templates? If the answer is yes, then this is a sign of QMS success.

3. Are control charts being utilized for every KPI? Are all leaders and stakeholders familiar with viewing data in these formats and understand what it means for data to be in or out of control? If so, the QMS is primed for success.

4. Do leaders understand their data, performance and outcomes over time? Are they sharing the data with stakeholders? Is this data tied back to their individual goals? Is non-goal attainment being escalated to the appropriate senior leaders? Is the governing body actively addressing non-goal attainment? If yes, this too is sign of success.

5. Are the main focal points of data display and interpretation goal attainment improving and in control? Simply put, is performance per KPI meeting goal, improving or in control? If yes to all these considerations, the QMS is successful from this perspective.

6. Do QMS leaders, senior leaders and governance leaders understand the data? Do they know the difference between normal variation and a crisis? Are they accountable for non-performance? Do these leaders report their data to QMS and up? If so, the QMS is primed for success.

7. Is the data readily available to all users from front-line staff to the governing body? Are common mechanisms such as communication boards, staff meetings, performance evaluation discussions with leaders/direct reports, etc. being regularly utilized in the organization's operating culture? If so, this too is a signal of QMS success.

Let's take a look at a practical exercise using run charts and control charts.

Scenario 1

Here leaders are reviewing outcomes for a quality metrics as noted in Figure 6.1. This figure represents a basic run chart over a three-year time period. The data points represent monthly measures of the quality metrics. The average line represents the average score for the metrics for each year. The goal line is the predetermined goal for the metrics.

There are three questions to answer.

1. Is the data meeting goal? As noted in the Figure 6.1, the data has improved over time. It did not meet goal for the first two years when comparing the average line to the goal line. But, for the last three months the metric's performance is above goal. On average for year three, the metrics is not meeting goal.

2. Is the data improving? Yes, the data has increased each year as evidenced by the average line increasing to goal. Thus, an improvement is indicated.

3. Is the data in or out of control? This will take a control chart. See Figure 6.2 for reference. The same data from the sample

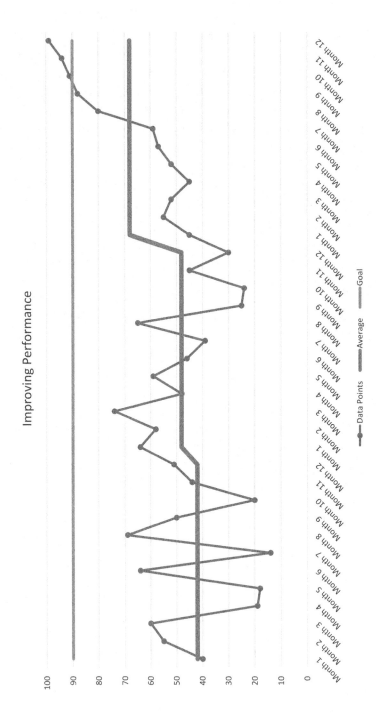

FIGURE 6.1
Sample run chart.

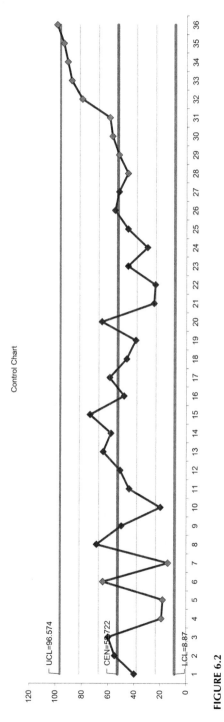

FIGURE 6.2
Sample control chart.

run chart in Figure 6.1 was analyzed in the control chart in Figure 6.2. Here, the data is out of control evidenced by the last six data points being above the average line and the last data point exceeding the upper control limit. Thus, special cause variation exists which is a signal something special is happening with this metrics outcomes.

So, how can a leader present this metrics to QMS leaders? Here is a sample report out:

- The quality metrics was analyzed in a run chart for the last three years. As noted in the graph, the outcomes have improved to goal each year. But, the metrics is still not meeting the goal for the last year. The data is also out of control as noted in the control chart. This means special cause variation is present which is a signal the data has improved with time.

Scenario 2

Here leaders are reviewing outcomes for a safety metrics as noted in Figure 6.3. This figure represents a basic run chart over a three-year time period. The data points represent monthly measures of the safety metrics. The average line represents the average score for the metrics for each year. The goal line is the predetermined goal for the metrics.

There are three questions to answer.

1. Is the data meeting goal? As noted in the Figure 6.3, the data is flat and has not improved over time. It did not meet goal for any of the three years when comparing the average line to the goal line.
2. Is the data improving? No, the data has not increased each year as evidenced by the average line not increasing to goal. The nature of outcomes is flat. Thus, an improvement is not indicated.
3. Is the data in or out of control? This will take a control chart. See Figure 6.4 for reference. The same data from the sample run chart in Figure 6.3 was analyzed in the control chart in Figure 6.4. Here, the data is in control, stable and predictable. Thus, current outcomes can be expected to continue unless QMS leader take aggressive actions and a different path forward.

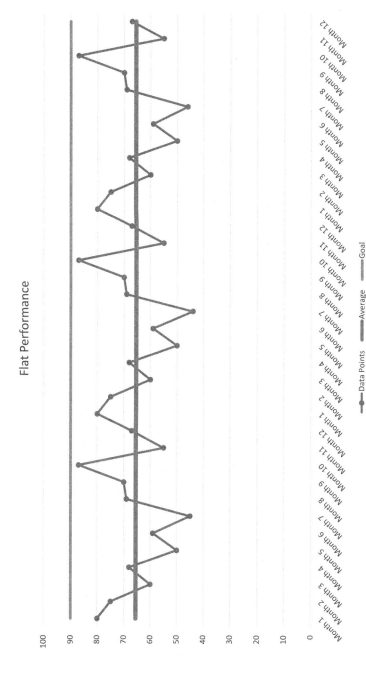

FIGURE 6.3
Sample run chart.

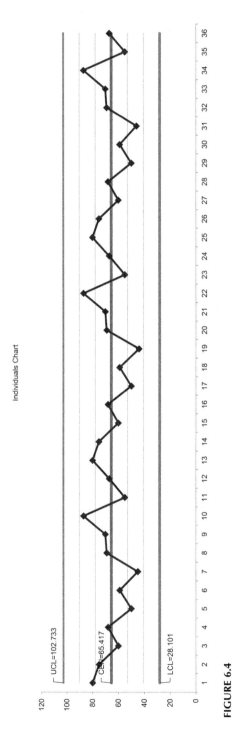

FIGURE 6.4
Sample control chart.

So, how can a leader present this metrics to QMS leaders? Here is a sample report out:

- The quality metrics was analyzed in a run chart for the last three years. As noted in the graph, the outcomes have been flat to goal over the three-year period. The metrics is still not meeting goal for any of the three years. The data is also in control, stable and predictable as noted in the control chart. This means current outcomes will continue unless leaders implement changes.

Scenario 3

Here, leaders are reviewing outcomes for a regulatory metrics compliance as noted in Figure 6.5. This figure represents a basic run chart over a three-year time period. The data points represent monthly measures of the quality metrics. The average line represents the average score for the metrics for each year. The goal line is the predetermined goal for the metrics.

There are three questions to answer.

1. Is the data meeting goal? As noted in the Figure 6.5, the data has declined over time. It did not meet goal for the first three years when comparing the average line to the goal line. On average for the three-year period, the metrics is not meeting goal.
2. Is the data improving? No, the data has not increased each year or any year as evidenced by the average line declining to goal. Thus, an improvement is not indicated.
3. Is the data in or out of control? This will take a control chart. See Figure 6.6 for reference. The same data from the sample run chart in Figure 6.5 was analyzed in the control chart in Figure 6.6. Here, the data is out of control evidenced by data points 10 and 21–29. Data point 10 exceeds the upper control limit and data points 21–29 represent a downward shift where six or more data points consecutively are located below the average line. Thus, special cause variation exists which is a signal something special is happening with this metrics outcomes.

So, how can a leader present this metrics to QMS leaders? Here is a sample report out:

- The quality metrics was analyzed in a run chart for the last three years. As noted in the graph, the outcomes have not improved to goal

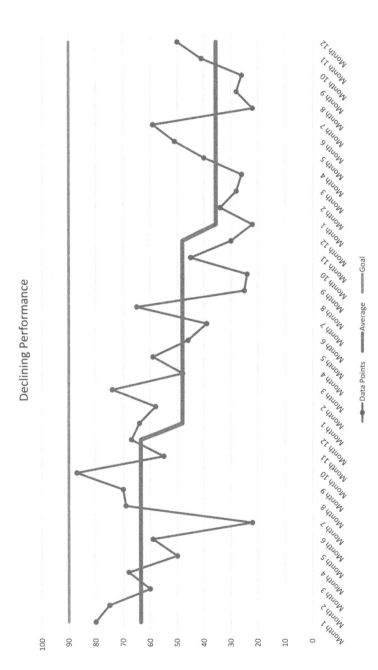

FIGURE 6.5
Sample run chart.

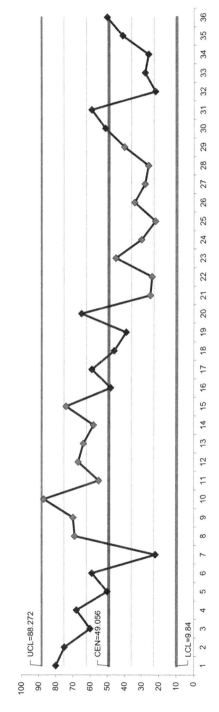

FIGURE 6.6
Sample control chart.

each year. The metrics is not meeting goal for any year. The data is also out of control as noted in the control chart. This means special cause variation is present which is a signal the QMS leaders must take immediate action to correct this outcome.

KNOWLEDGE TRANSFER

One major measure of success for a QMS model is the knowledge it possesses, creates, develops, cultivates and shares. As we noted in previous chapters, knowledge sharing is synonymous with knowledge transfer. The question at hand is how the organization, and particularly the QMS, share knowledge from one person to another, across the enterprise and externally.

1. Does the QMS create best practices, innovative ideas and improvements that are published in industry-respective venues?
2. Do QMS leaders present their successes in industry best practice venues?
3. Has the QMS knowledge been 'codified' or simply published in books that contribute to the industry body of knowledge?
4. Do QMS leaders represent the QMS outcomes in other industry venues outside of the organization's technical expertise?

If the answer to these considerations is yes, then knowledge transfer is also a measure of success.

SUMMARY

The takeaway is that QMS has several measures of success as noted in the previous discussion. Unfortunately, a good conversation or meeting for the sake of meeting does not qualify for a measure of success. Successful QMS models are associated with data improvements, knowledge sharing, a structure that resonates with stakeholders and produces outcomes, a process that identifies and solves problems and governance that is accountable and results-oriented. If these measures of success are present and aligned with the organization's culture, then the QMS has the greatest chance to succeed.

7

Case Study: Is QMS a Risky Proposition?

Risk can be defined as, 'the possibility of something bad happening.' [1] In layman's terms, risk is the probability that an endeavor may fail or succeed. The key is that risk is bad and should be eliminated at every turn. But, this concept begs several questions.

Can leaders leverage risk to succeed? Does the presence of risk mean ultimate failure? Can leaders use simple risk tools to measure, mitigate and control their risks? Will risk disrupt leaders and their operations if not identified and corrected? Will leaders understand their risk levels if they don't measure risk? We will answer these and other considerations in the following.

The reality is that risk is correlated with change. As change grows, so does risk. In our world today, change is the new normal and only constant. Thus, leaders must be prepared for, equipped to handle and master the art and science of risk mitigation. If not, disruption is all but certain.

CASE IN POINT

A thought leader was engaged by a large service organization that was experiencing operational declines. For years, the enterprise was a high performer in its industry. As time passed, the organization experienced several leadership restructures. With each restructure, change increased and so did risk. Moreover, the cyclical changes created massive disruptions that contributed to the organization's operational decline.

The first order of business by the thought leader was an assessment of the enterprise. During the discovery phase of the assessment, the thought leader

DOI: 10.4324/9781003485131-7

focused on structure and process. The organization touted a well-organized and effective governance structure. When the thought leader asked for a one-page schematic of the governance model, none was available. Also, the thought leader interviewed several top leaders who could not speak fluently about the governance model. Thus, governance existed in theory only.

Next, the thought leader completed a data review. This analysis included a historical review of the organization's value metrics such as quality scores, costs, customer satisfaction, safety metrics and the like. The leader focused on three basic attributes. Over time were the KPIs (key performance indicators) meeting goal, improving to goal and in or out of control.

The data review was simple, quick and very effective. To display the data, the thought leader utilized simple run charts and control charts. The analysis revealed interesting trends to say the least. The organization had five large business units. Each had its own individual governance structure and quality management system (QMS) model. Of the five business units, less than half were meeting their value metrics over several years. The range of outcomes for all units was 60%. Simply put, there was a lot of variation in value metrics goal attainment. In this case, variation is bad and should be eliminated at every turn.

On further review, less than 40% of the metrics for all business units combined were showing any sign of improvement. The startling finding related to control. Less than 10% of the metrics for all units combined were in control. This simply meant that over 90% of the KPIs were out of control, unstable and bridled with special cause variation. Typically, the more control organizations have with their outcomes, the more stable and predictable the operation will be.

The assessment then shifted to the QMS models. As noted there were five different models as evidence by their structure and process. Five QMS models were structured differently, had various data display techniques and lacked standardization on every front. The organization simply had a silo approach to QMS where each business unit marched to the beat of its own drum.

During leadership interviews, the thought leader asked several leaders independently to describe the QMS process for each business unit. Also, the leader asked those being interviewed if they could display their QMS model in a single schematic or one-page document. The answer to these questions was simply no. The organization's leaders could not fluently describe the QMS model, its processes, how it tied into the governance model and could not present the structure or processes in a single slide. Thus, QMS was a theory only.

The thought leader quickly realized the organization was out of control, the downward spiral would continue and there was no objective evidence that improvements were working. Outcomes were missing because structure and process were ineffective. The leader packaged the findings with other statistical evidence and later presented the findings to a group of top leaders.

The thought leader presumed all leaders would be excited of the findings. In reality, the conversation did not go as plans. Some leaders of various business units agreed that outcomes were less than desired. But, the source of the declines became a hot button issue. These leaders began a laundry list of suspected root causes such as turnover, staff engagement issues, limited financial resources and the like. Although some of the issues were viable operational challenges, the leadership cadre missed the point.

The organization lacked the basic attributes to succeed. This lack of structure and process related to governance and QMS were the lynch pins of the organization's operational declines. To further support this assertion, the thought leaders prepared a risk-based assessment for the leadership cadre. The purpose was to help the leaders see the big picture through a risk-based lens.

QMS Risk Levels

The leader began with an overview of Figure 7.1.

There are four major risk levels as these relate to QMS. The lowest organizational risk of not having a proper QMS or governance structure

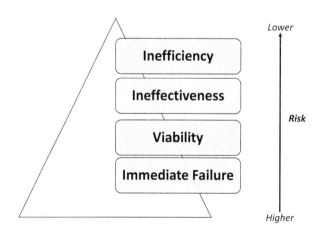

FIGURE 7.1
QMS risk levels.

is inefficiency. Here, leaders and stakeholders arduously spend large amounts of time in meetings or other activities entertaining the organization's value challenges. Inefficient QMS models simply imply that more resources than needed are dedicated to the QMS structure or process. The problem with this risk is that QMS should be action forward and focused. Thus, leaders should spend less time meeting, talking, etc. and more time acting upon or fixing issues.

The next level of QMS risk is ineffectiveness. An ineffective QMS can be spotted a mile away by the trained eye. The single greatest indicator is outcomes. If value metrics such as quality, cost, customer satisfaction and the like fail to meet goals or improve over long periods of time, then arguably the QMS and overarching governance models are ineffective.

The third level of risk is viability. Will the QMS be viable in years to come? This is predicated on the structure, process, outcomes, market direction and the organization's true north (as discussed in previous chapter). A simple rule of thumb or gauge to answer this question is as follows:

- Does the QMS produced consistent goal attainment for value metrics over long periods of time?
- Does the QMS improve value metrics over time?
- Does QMS ensure high levels of value metrics control?

If the answer to any of these three considerations is no, then QMS viability is in question and high-risk proposition.

The highest risk for QMS is immediate failure. There are several contributing factors here. One, QMS models can fail immediately if they are not structured properly. Two, a lack of an effective QMS process will lead to failure. Three, QMS failure is a high risk when top organizational leaders don't know their risk, understand the QMS process and are not accountable for QMS outcomes. Four, QMS models fail when other stakeholders outside top leadership are not aware of the QMS, don't understand its purpose and cannot relate to its functions. Simply put, it does not resonate with stakeholders day to day work.

The thought leader's assessment revealed that some of the QMS models for the business units were at high risk for various reasons. Some of the QMS models were simply inefficient. Leaders here spent countless hours in needless meetings and conversations talking about problems instead of solving them. The adage of 'a waste of time' applied here.

Other QMS models in the organization were ineffective. Here, the QMS leaders experienced years of value metrics goal attainment declines without correction. Thus, the QMS and governance models were not aligned for success. The adage of 'spiraling out of control' applied here. Most of the KPIs were not meeting goal, out of control and not corrected by the QMS.

One QMS model was an immediate risk of failure. Leaders in this business unit could not speak about the QMS structure, its processes and could not accurately interpret the data. Simply put, the house was on fire (operationally speaking) and they didn't know it. In short, QMS was ineffective and simply a waste of time.

Overall, the thought leader revealed that the QMS for the enterprise was not viable. The long-term chance of the organization succeeding in this environment was zero. A restructure was warranted. The only question was when, not if.

QMS Risk Matrix

The thought leader then leveraged a risk matrix for the conversation with the organization's leaders. See Figure 7.2 for details.

Here, the leaders simply risk assessed two attributes: QMS structure and outcomes. The outcomes were scored from low to high. The structure was assessed to being basic or advanced.

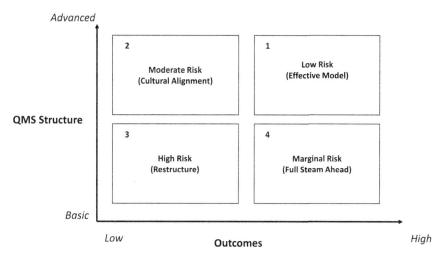

FIGURE 7.2
QMS risk matrix.

There are four quadrants or boxes in the risk matrix. Box 1 represents a low-risk proposition. Here, the QMS structure is advanced and the outcomes are high. Simply put, the QMS has a scalable structure, consistently high outcomes and can be used in any arena. Thus, it's effective, low risk and good model for leaders to employ.

Box 2 represents moderate risk. Here, the QMS model is advanced. If needed leaders could scale the model over multiple business units. But, the outcomes are low. This calls for cultural alignment. In simplest of terms, QMS leaders must ensure stakeholders at all levels understand the QMS, can speak about it fluently, understand the data and can relate the QMS process to their daily work. If this is accomplished, there is a good probability for success. If not, risk could disrupt the model.

Box 3 represents the highest risk to QMS. Here, the structure is basic. In most instances, a basic QMS is a silo model where it fits certain business model types and may be limited in scalability. Also, the outcomes are low. Thus, leaders in this scenario would consider restructuring the QMS model for better outcomes, scalability across various business units and long-term viability.

Box 4 represents marginal risk. In this scenario, the QMS structure is basic. In contrast, the outcomes are high which is ideal. Leaders would continue full steam ahead with the QMS model and adjust the structure or processes if needed. The adage of 'if it's not broken, don't fix it' applies here. The only consideration is if the QMS is viable long-term. Simply put, is the structure going to continue produce high-level outcomes of the organization's strategy or market position change? If the answer is no, then the risk should be mitigated with structural upgrades.

Leveraging this tool for the five business units, the thought leader displayed that three of the QMS models were at high risk. Simply put, a restructure was in order. Two were at marginal risk as they met a reasonable amount of value metrics goals, but had a lot of variation in goal attainment over the time. Therefore, some improvement was needed to gain more control in outcomes. The takeaway is that the risk matrix revealed the organization's risk proposition was high and the QMS models needed work. Otherwise, operational outcomes would continue to decline.

QMS Risk Assessment Tool

The thought leader then took the assessment one step further with Figure 7.3.

QMS Model	Structure 1-Silo 2- One Size Fits All	Process 1- Ineffective 2-Effective	Outcomes 1- < 50% Goals Attained 2- 50%-80% Goals Attained 3- > 80% Goals Attained	Stakeholder Satisfaction 1- < 50% Satisfied 2- 50%-80% Satisfied 3- > 80% Satisfied	Standardized 1-No 2-Yes	Cultural Alignment 1-Not Aligned 2-Aligned	Risk Score *Sum Columns 2-7 Lower Score = Higher Risk	Risk Level	QMS Plan
QMS Model 1	1	1	1	1	1	1	6	High Risk	Restructure
QMS Model 2	2	2	2	2	2	2	12	Low Risk	Viable Model
QMS Model 3	1	2	1	1	1	2	8	High Risk	Restructure
QMS Model 4	2	1	3	1	1	2	10	Average Risk	Caution
QMS Model 5	2	1	1	3	1	1	9	High Risk	Restructure
Avg Score	1.6	1.4	1.6	1.6	1.2	1.6			
Risk Level	High Risk	High Risk	High Risk	High Risk	High Risk	High Risk			

FIGURE 7.3
QMS risk tool.

The risk tool was used to assess each QMS model on six attributes: structure, process, outcomes, stakeholder satisfaction, standardization and cultural alignment. The structure measurement was as previously discussed. Did the QMS have basic structural components such as inputs, a process, outputs and governance or oversight? Silo or business unit model specific structures are higher risk than a scalable one-size-fits-all model.

The process is rated as ineffective or effective. An ineffective QMS process is higher risk than its counterpart. In short, does the QMS have a process to filter out issues related to value, service, cost and quality as a starter? Does the process entail the assignment of performance improvement practitioners to solve the issues? Does the process produce measurable, significant and sustainable improvements? Does the QMS process require continuous improvement after the initial wins or improvements are achieved?

The next risk attribute assessed is outcomes or goal attainment. If the QMS meets less than 50% of its goals, it's the highest risk proposition. 50% to 80% goal attainment is moderate risk. A QMS that can meet greater than 80% of its value metrics goals is lowest risk.

The leader then included stakeholder satisfaction in the risk assessment tool. Here, QMS models were rated on satisfaction rates of the stakeholders involved in or leading the QMS for each business unit. Those QMS models that had stakeholder satisfaction rates less than 50% are highest risk. 50% to 80% satisfaction rates are moderate risk. A QMS with stakeholder satisfaction greater than 80% is lowest risk.

Next, the thought leader assessed standardization. Was the QMS standardized in structure, process, attendees, accountability mechanisms, templates, agendas, meeting minutes, data display and the like? When standardization was lacking, the risk was higher. When QMS models were standardized, the risk was lower and they tended to be more effective.

Finally, each QMS model was assessed on cultural alignment. The test here was simple. Could leaders speak about the QMS model? Was the model displayed in a single schematic or slide? Did all stakeholders understand the purpose of QMS, their role in the process and how it is related to their daily work? When culture is aligned, risk is lower and vice versa.

As noted in Figure 7.3, three of the five QMS models were high risk. Thus, a restructure was warranted. One of QMS models was low risk and a viable model. The remaining model was average risk due to process, standardization and stakeholder satisfaction opportunities. Thus, improvement efforts were in order. But, this model had potential to improve easily.

SUMMARY

So, what did we learn from the overview of QMS risk? One, QMS is a risky business. Not all QMS models, processes or outcomes are the same. Two, leaders must measure to understand their risk. Simple risk tools, as noted, are viable outlets for leaders to measure, risk assess, prioritize, mitigate and prevent risk from existing. But, how will leaders know the risk to their QMS models if it's not measured? Simply put, they won't. Three, in order for QMS models to be effective they at minimum require structure, process and outcomes that ensure viability long-term.

The takeaway is that change is the new normal and only constant in today's environment. As change grows, so does risk. Thus, leaders must assess, prioritize and mitigate risks successfully to succeed with QMS. If not, QMS will exist in theory only and the organization will ultimately fail.

NOTE

1. Wikipedia, 2022

Conclusion

Often leaders struggle with the concept of Quality Management System (QMS). Unfortunately, they fail to understand this concept, implement ineffective QMS models and subsequently are disrupted from their roles. More important and even more impactful are the consequences a poorly designed and executed QMS model has on organizational stakeholders including customers.

There are several reasons leaders struggle with QMS. One, their organization has an ineffective governance model. Two, the QMS model itself is lacking key components and is ineffective. Three, leaders don't understand their data. The data display phenomena occurs when leaders fail to use basic tools such as run charts and control charts to determine if outcomes are improving or in and out of control.

Thus, perception is often not reality. Leaders don't know what they don't measure properly. In some instances, the QMS is effective when leaders make changes they should not. In other instances, the QMS is out of control, leaders don't know it and they fail to act when a crisis has emerged. This lack of insight and knowledge contribute to high levels of disruption. Therefore, leaders are crushed by the operational waves that they should be riding if the QMS was effective.

In today's world, change is the new normal and only constant. In many industries, such as healthcare for example, the foundations of the industries themselves are shaking greater than any other time in history. As change grows, so does the associated risk and disruption. How will leaders and their organizations succeed in high-risk environments without a good foundation? The short answer is they won't. The starting point for success is QMS.

At the end of the day, leaders and their organizations succeed or fail based on the outcomes that are achieved. Effective leaders are those who understand their risk, plan ahead, solve problems, mitigate risks, sustain wins and transform organizational outcomes in high-risk environments via a well-defined and functional QMS model. Their counterparts quickly become the center of focus for the next case study or book.

DOI: 10.4324/9781003485131-8

Do you know your risk? Is your QMS effective? Can you visually display your QMS model in one slide? If you were asked, can you accurately describe your organization's governance model? Can your organization's stakeholders accurately describe and relate to the QMS? Do they regularly see accurate data displaying improvements and signaling crises? Is your QMS standardized with templates, agendas, A3s and the like? Are improvement resources readily available for and active in addressing opportunities identified by the QMS? Can you produce a list of measurable and significant improvements tied directly to value metrics? Finally, is your organization sharing its knowledge and QMS successes in industry best practice venues?

If you can answer yes to all these questions, you're well prepared to leverage QMS for success. If not, leverage the principles and insight in this book to ensure your QMS is effective, aligned for success and ready for the next challenge.

Index

Note: Locators in *italics* represent figures.

Printed in the United States
by Baker & Taylor Publisher Services